Notes on
an Emergency

*For Pat –
a professional and
personal comrade...,
Egbeth*

Notes on an Emergency

A Journal of Recovery

ELIZABETH LÉONIE SIMPSON

W. W. NORTON & COMPANY · NEW YORK · LONDON

Library of Congress Cataloging in Publication Data

Simpson, Elizabeth Léonie.
Notes on an emergency.

1. Meninges—Tuberculosis—Patients—United
States—Biography. 2. Simpson, Elizabeth Léonie
I. Title.
RC312.5.M45S57   1982   362.1'9699581'00924 [B]
ISBN 0-393-01514-9   81-18760

W. W. Norton & Company, Inc. 500 Fifth Avenue, New York, N. Y. 10110
W. W. Norton & Company Ltd. 37 Great Russell Street, London WC1B 3NU

1 2 3 4 5 6 7 8 9 0

FOR MY FAMILY

*. . . a book should serve as the
axe for the frozen sea within us.*

—*KAFKA*

CONTENTS

x ∫ Contents

FOREWORD

This is a story of courage and the indomitable will of a human being to live. That night when she was found by a watchman sick, weeping, and helpless in a parking lot, Elizabeth Simpson seemed, in her family's mind, to have a serious case of flu. But as she got worse, the ailment turned out to be tubercular meningitis, a disease in which the fatality rate is 94 percent. Elizabeth, who had been a published poet, scholar, and university teacher, regressed into hallucinations with the strange ecstasy that accompanies this state. She then went into coma, where she remained in prenatal unconsciousness for a number of weeks. The doctors in the hospital where she was in intensive care pronounced her dying, and this was the message that those of us around the country who knew her, however briefly, heard.

When she finally came out of the coma, she was unable to think or to speak, and her hearing and sight were radically impaired. One aspect of this heroic story is how her family and relatives and friends rallied round to aid her, a picture which restores one's faith in human caring in such a time of dire need.

In these months she had no past because she had no memory, no future, and no present. She went through what many of us have written about but very few have experienced so directly—sheer nothingness. Looking back on it later, she writes, contrary to Descartes, "I could not think, but I still was: I continued to be—even with an empty, malfunctioning mind —and I know it."

The long, painful climb back to the point where she could use her mind and her body was to me the most absorbing part of the story. "Waiting, hoping and despairing, being and doubting—these were the years of recovery. Except for the first few months I was home from the hospital, the waiting has not been static, not negative; it has burgeoned and has been amplified with hope, even when my rational mind denied its rationality."

I recall that summer a psychologist, a friend of Elizabeth's and mine, was visiting me in New Hampshire. He had just heard that Elizabeth was out of the coma, and he stated that she now needed to be taught all over again the basic skills of life. Her synapses could be reconnected, he explained, and he flew out to California to help her achieve that purpose.

After some months, she writes, "I had begun to be rebellious and, hence, affirmative." Her anger also returned and with it her vitality. She learned that anger can be constructive, and is a crucial part of survival, and that "self-pity can be a fatal disease in itself." "Knowing I am doomed, I may have to expect it, but I will never accept it." As I read these sentences, the line from Dylan Thomas kept running through my mind: "Rage, rage against the dying of the light."

Hearing she was on the mend, we invited her to participate in a small conference to explore the theory of humanistic psychology. She writes about this:

The two-day meeting was held in a garden hotel within the city; each time I stepped from my room I was lost—lost in the dining room, in the entrance, and, after dark or during the day, crossing the garden to get from meeting place to meeting place. The limits of the space in which I was operating cognitively were about four feet in each direction from my physical presence. No maps beyond that were possible. I did not want to be spoken to because I could not reply. Why? Aside from the vast lacunae of words, I simply did not remember what had just been said to me!

She is grateful that she received the best medical care available, but there is a clear statement of the insufficiency of medicine as such. "Beyond a certain point, medical practitioners did not help my transition back to full functioning—because their professional interest and training were simply too narrow." Her father, an eminent scientist in Cambridge, had come out to see her, and, believing the statements of the scientific medical personnel that she was dying in her coma, he had then left. One gets from this book a stronger conviction that no matter how great our science becomes, it can never encompass the invisible power of the human will to recovery.

The book predicts the future way to health, which she happened upon by accident, as "holistic health," which treats the whole person, focusing upon preventative medicine, anticipating threats of disease, and maintaining health rather than being compelled to restore it—"Health is abundance. Not simply the absence of illness or disease. It is the experience of plenty, of strength and vitality, of actualized possibility."

One turns to ultimate thoughts in such a crisis, and Elizabeth Simpson, when her inner faculties returned, had time to ponder such considerations. She worked out her own brand of existentialism, which includes one's need for family and friends. "Some of us can pretend that we owe nothing to anyone, but survivors know we need each other."

God to her is one who "permits me to find my own way. . . . I believe in this God. But not with certitude, not beyond a reasonable doubt. . . . Perhaps the task is not really to find answers, but to learn how to live with the questions.

"I believe that I have come into touch with ultimate reality. I do not believe in immortality, in life after death in the conventional sense, but I do believe in an indestructible and timeless core within each personality."

Is it this timeless core that she is showing us in this book? Her body is still partially crippled, and she falls, but less and less frequently and less painfully, and she knows that "being a cripple is not a physical state; it is a way of thinking about yourself." Mentally she seems wholly renewed. She has redis-covered her poetry—the proof of which is that she has given us this beautiful, poetic book. —Rollo May

ACKNOWLEDGMENTS

Four years in the making, this book was lived as therapeutic self-expression. Some who shared that experience are named within it; here are a few of the many others who influenced its final form: Edwin Barker, George I. and Judith Brown, Mary Cunnane, Jeannette Hopkins, Richard Jones, Peter Scharf, and John Wurr.

Notes on
an Emergency

PROLOGUE

Ah! must—
Designer infinite!—
Ah! must Thou char the wood ere Thou canst
limn with it?

—FRANCIS THOMPSON

My name is Elizabeth, but if you call me Ishmael, as an analogy it would be accurate enough. Like that grand teller of tales, I have sailed, watching Ahab and Moby Dick—the eternal powers of good and evil—engage in allegoric battle. I have translated such tension and strength to the forces competing within me, forces of health and of disease, and I am building an image in testament to that new, inward domain. Like Ishmael, I am the sole survivor and so must share the story, if it is to be told. But, unlike him, I draw on others, on participants and observers, since, as teller, I could neither be accurate nor neutral: the path inward and back into the past is a map I can no longer draw with veracity even today, some years after the event. (I will draw on others, but I do agree with historian James MacGregor Burns that it is *authenticity*, not *accuracy*, that is most important in reporting real events.)

After a shaking, shaping experience there is a need to put

3

oneself in question, to do it personally, and to avoid the cate-
gorization, generalization, and pronouncement making of traditional science. Benjamin Disraeli wrote that biography is life
without theory. That is what I am trying to describe in this
partial life history. I am presenting *my* impressions, *my* bias,
my slant when I can. And when I can't, I rely on those of
others.

It is true that knowing events and change only by report can
make reaction to them feel inauthentic. But the world can't be
seen without distortion. Even enlightened philosophers or the
mellowed and experienced aged do not have an unobstructed
view through a window wide open. We see what we know more
readily than we know what we see; we are more constructive
than realistic. Social scientists have regretted publicly that they
no more than the rest of us could know directly the life of
anyone but themselves. Truth lies within each of us. But after
my illness I could not know that of myself. I could no longer
refer to the source. Is what I'm saying truthful? Insofar as I
remember—but that is not very far. But, then, does subjective
inquiry ever yield the whole truth, even when memory holds?

The other writers included here do not speak for me but,
rather, for themselves—although I believe there is a semblance
of consistency in their observations and opinions. The reader
is the listener to this collection of speeches and must do his or
her own intake and elaboration. Scientists may systematically
observe, collect, and analyze data, but only artists record the
truth—a personal reaction to experience in a particular social
situation from which the reader can take what he or she finds
insightful or useful. I am both researcher and artist here, trying
to construct a social reality as well as a personal one. We all
seek to know how life is led by others, but even more so how
it is led by ourselves, or has been. Somehow, publicized "fact"
becomes undeniable, incontestable. Perhaps, for me, publica-

tion will bring certainty in place of vacuity and tentativeness.

I am trying to reactivate energies sleeping within past skills, to put them to work again. Hunger for high cause and personal achievement has been transmuted into longing for the brief accomplishments possible from day to day. These efforts at writing are attempts to recover, through the open nerves of intimate feelings, memories that illness (not time) has effectively obliterated. When the blanks in knowledge occur or the "facts" are messy and contradictory, the edges of falsification become blurred and the territory more comely. Nonfiction reporting is always the weaving of patterns of memory, records, and prose in an attempt to transform the past, to cull and prune it—to keep the city "tidy," as English candy wrappers admonish the eater.

Perhaps I should write an article or book about how I wrote this book. There has been nothing linear about it—from conception to conclusion. Order has been incidental to the need for expression and the rowdy, inhibiting difficulty of achieving it. At times, the meaty bones in the stew of frustration and anger have been hard to find. In a recent interview Norman Mailer suggested that, if the words stir the writer too much, they won't stir anyone who reads them. One must keep one's distance even from self-examination and the personal.

I awakened in what seemed a strange land with few of the key words and phrases in what had been my native tongue. I had to learn how to speak and how to communicate. I had no knowledge of how I got where I am *now* or where I had been before. And so, for several years, I have been writing my own oral history, talking to family, to friends, to people who knew me and who were willing to tell me who I was before my illness or, at least, who I had been to them. If the person who lives today is writing these words, it is because their constituent parts have been made accessible by those who knew me in the past. Those people have provided the personal past, the past of impressions and interactions; and my own carefully preserved records—journals, reprints, letters, files of clippings and notes—have supplied a type of objectivity. I had married young, still in college, had raised my three children essentially alone, and had become a high-school teacher of Spanish and English so that I could have the same working hours that my children had at school. Later, I shifted professional gears radically by taking a mid-life doctoral degree from the University of California at Berkeley, followed by a year of specialized training in developmental psychology at the University of Southern California, where I had become associate director of the Center for International Education. All of my life I have written—during some seasons more of one kind of work than another: poetry, fiction, essays on education and moral development which appeared as journal articles or as chapters in others' books, social-science textbooks or research reports on adolescent political beliefs or the growth of humanistic education in American schools. These published records, these precious words, have given me access to that unknown person living in vanished lands: myself.

Life is more than the sum of words; but words strive after reality, help us to define it, and give it value. Why does a writer record if it is not to cheat fate, to hinder oblivion, to share and, therefore, to extend experience? Writing is the building of a relationship between the author/maker and the reader; it is a lessening of the distance between each person who suffers and the mind which reports or creates accounts of these sufferings. Direct confrontation of the suffering of others changes a person forever. The doors of possibility are suddenly widened. To write about despair or illness honestly is to begin to conquer them. It is not the event itself that is being communicated, but its acquisition and disposition by the participant, creative mind.

Personal expression in any mode flounders before painful, sovereign reality. Viewed as fantasy, it does not have to be confronted; but, as the record of experience, it creates another situation entirely: the fantasy is real, yet the observer, shaken, may have no means of evaluating its dimensions. When you are trying to understand what is there, everyday life can include too much reality and art not include enough to do more than hint at it. Writing, as a medium of art, is an intervention as well as a means of communication. I am trying to build my life today—not just to *re*construct it—by intervening in that reality. As Pirandello wrote, "A fact is like a sack; it won't stand up till you've put something in it."

Surely it is a myth that death or conversion is necessary in order to experience metaphoric "rebirth." For most people, life is a process of continual psychological disjunction, of beginning over and over again. What happened to me was just an extreme case. What came through to me was only hints and wisps of the reality "out there," and I felt like closing into myself even further in order to protect myself from what I could not reach outside. If it was not accessible, I could not afford to value it —or even to be aware of it. But the gradual acceptance of emptiness without panic made it possible for me to be "filled" as I mended. (All by myself I have been a developing nation.) And it has been in the empty spaces—the lacunae, vacuums, interstices, pauses, voids, black holes in inner territories—that new things have begun. We still know too little about what happens after physical or psychological breakdown, what the possibility of chemical recombinations and the formation of new patterns of behavior are.

I am still discovering the pattern of that past being of mine; and, although some pieces are more easily identified than others, overall there is a disjunctive, patchwork quality to the product: everyone's image, every person's contributed memory is unique in texture, depth, and design. Although there is some consensual reality, these perceptions often differ and so the "facts" differ. Is there really a hard core of fact that exists objectively and independently of the interpretation of the recorder? Some historians, like Edward Hallet Carr, believe this to be a preposterous fallacy. Legend has it that history tells us what happened and fiction tells how it felt.

As I put this personal history together, disparities make raw edges, overlaps, or gaps in the model that I am building. When these facts do not agree with each other, I have only one way of knowing what is "true": the feelings that arise, persistent and undeniable, informing me what my emotional reactions to an incident had been long after the happening itself has been wiped away. Its meaning outlives the event. Writing is a way of dealing with the self that one has not made but has been presented with—a way to access and understanding.

While much of my personal history has been culled from others' hoards, an important part of it has never left me: what I can't remember visually or verbally I can resurrect in that breathless area between the ribs, where feeling lives. Tell me who you are, and, although I may not remember your name or how our lives crossed paths, I will instantly know whether I feared, admired, loved, or was bored by you.

Why did I become ill? I would be more comfortable if it could be explained simply, physiologically. It should be easy to resist the kind of generalization that Simonton, Mathews-Simonton, and Creighton* have built out of their studies of cancer victims, but it isn't. From the descriptions (provided by others) of my life during the year before I fell ill, I am sure that I had at least some of these initiating attributes. Certainly, I

---

*Carl Simonton, Stephanie Matthews-Simonton, and James Creighton, *Getting Well Again* (Los Angeles: Tarcher, 1978).

believe that I was chronically worried, depressed, and hostile. Here are the five steps of a psychological process that they believe frequently precedes cancer:

1. experiences in childhood resulting in decisions to be a certain kind of person and, therefore, limiting the resources for coping with stresses;
2. a cluster of stressful life events;
3. a stress-instigated problem with which the individual does not know how to cope;
4. belief that one is a victim because unchangeable rules prevent the problem from being solved;
5. distance placed between the problem and the self so that the individual becomes static, unchanging, and rigid.

Such an individual has become hopeless prior to the disease. He or she has been running in place without meaning, living out a process that does not *cause* cancer but, rather, *permits* it to develop. The next paragraph filled me with an intense sense of recognition and of shame:

> The crucial point to remember is that all of us create the *meaning* of events in our lives. The individual who assumes the victim stance *participates* by assigning meanings to life events that prove there is no hope. Each of us *chooses*—although not always at a conscious level—how we are going to react. The intensity of the stress is determined by the meaning we assign to it and the rules we have established for how we will cope with stress.

Can desperate sickness be *sought* as a practical way to obtain peace of mind? As the only possibility? A way of gaining permission to cop out? And is quitting the maintenance of health a means of resignation—to avoid coruscating, dead-ended hope as well as personal responsibility? These are only some of the questions I have met along the way.

One final note. There is, for many of us, some uneasiness associated with the public exposure of private parts. Yet a biography with any interest at all is necessarily revealing and divulging. A growing social ethic seems to support this practice, whatever the reasons behind its accomplishment. My own experiences have been told not to harrow but to strengthen others. I have felt the need to bear witness, to share the sense that what has happened to me should not be clouded over by an illusion of separateness. What I have learned is not mine alone, nor can it be. There is, then, a need to reveal; but with it there is also a need to protect and withhold. The deeper the theme, the more complicated it is to include other themes that are collateral to it.

Here, then, is the tract of that invisible path leading to the lost body of the past.

Part One

1

THE UNCONSCIOUS,
THE UNKNOWN

O reader,
When all of you stirs as you read me,
It is I who am stirring within you.

—MIGUEL DE UNAMUNO

The summer of 1974 was an extraordinary one for me. I had just finished a report for the Ford Foundation on the growth and shape of humanistic education in the United States and, abandoning the compulsive, workaholic habits of the professional freelancer, had taken a backpacking vacation with the Sierra Club on the Kenai Peninsula in Alaska. In the past, I had done some river running on the Stanislaus and, during one early college summer, had been cook for a New Mexican paleontological expedition encamped between mesas in the striated desert. Camping was not new to me, but the Alaskan venture was different. For two weeks I was to be constantly on the go, surrounded—in four dimensions it seemed—by the incredible and awesome mountains I had encountered for the first time earlier that year when I had viewed them from the towns and cities where visiting colleagues and I were taking part in community-oriented programs, sponsored by the Na-

13

tional Endowment for the Humanities. I had left the state determined to return—not to the strong and autonomous people who had made us so welcome, but to the eternal challenge of the sculptured land itself, so remote, absolute, and indifferent.

I remember nothing of this today, but in my files are the letters and the United States Geological Survey maps on which I had plotted that canoe and foot journey, a plot that included the twenty-four-hour detour to Watch Mountain and along the Killey River, where I and a knowledgeable companion were lost, with no dread at all and certainly no sense of irretrievability, from our small group of campers. Unconsciously integrated, the beauty and the wonder of that experience—like that of other forgotten episodes of past strength and positive awareness—later helped me to re-create a destroyed personality.

Returning to my professional life at the end of that trip was crossing the boundaries into another culture. I was suddenly melancholy. Feeling disoriented, I went east to see people at Ford, attend meetings, and visit family. The depression was lasting too long; even with interesting work and good company I was unable to shake it off. I began to realize (as my sister had, long before I knew it) that I was not always making sense when I talked. When I got home to Santa Monica, my younger daughter Bethany, who lived with me while she was going to UCLA, insisted that I see the doctor, and I did, for the first time, on the twentieth of October. Nothing seemed to be seriously amiss. He suggested a psychologist and some therapy; I was obviously extremely fatigued.

But the decision was no longer mine. The extraordinary had already become ordinary. A typical example occurred one day when I parked my car, as usual, in the university lot and, when the time came to look for it, could not find it. That evening

I, who had never cried in public in my life, wandered among the vehicles, streaming tears until the security guard spotted me and came over to help. (The car, of course, was where I had left it—not fifteen feet from where I stood.)

The episode was a symptom and a meaningful one. I know about it today only because I had told the incident to a friend before I got worse. For many of us much of the past is inaccessible, either unrecorded or unremembered. But it happened and it mattered. Even without memory, its unrecognized effects live on in reactions to daily occurrences in the present and will affect the future as well.

Seven years ago I came down with tubercular meningitis. Intuitive, systematic diagnosis saved my life (although 6-percent survival rate is par for the course), but within a desperate month I had lost my balance, my memory, much of my hearing and eyesight, as well as my capacity to speak, to read, and to think. Pushed by my adult children, seventy-three pounds of static and empty life went home from the hospital in a wheelchair, barely able to stand and completely unable to recognize the well-wishers who called.

Although much of my past is still gone, it is easier now for me to return to this history, to re-enter it. The light of these mending years has been softened; the stars are, once more, within the range of imagination, if no longer within the reach of my body's eyes. Discourse with family and friends has cured the past, electromagnetically lifting the heaps of steel rubble between its happening and my consciousness. What I have wanted to write, recovering from a sustained and serious illness, is a useful book and a radiant one, showering the light of a life —my own—that would not be put out casually, as with the flick of a switch. Like all home-grown, well-socialized philosophers and scientists, I have searched for meaning and for understanding. I want to share that search. I want to tell what

happened and more: I want to explore whether it mattered—
not because it was *I,* but because, since it *was* I, it could be
others. The experience was my own; its meaning was not.

My earlier life was not irretrievable; the annihilation of
conscious experience—the eternal forgetting—did not last
forever, after all. But change took place. As Robert Jay Lifton
and Eric Olson* have written, "The profoundest insight is
attainable only by the survivor: he who has touched death in
some bodily or psychic way and has himself remained alive."
These writers cite the theologian and poet John Donne's belief:
there are given biological events—universals—in human life,
but these events elicit personal meanings and responses that
are individually chosen. So it was with me.

Several years ago, determined to lay out this record, I sat
down with my TB specialist and reviewed the stages of attack
and their degree (to which I still have no access of memory).
Shortly after the parking-lot episode, I began to experience
pleuritic chest pains and early symptoms of pneumonia. Soon
I had a temperature that wavered up over 103 degrees; I hurt
behind my eyes and on the top of my head. A thick yellow
discharge flowed from my right ear. On the thirtieth of October, the doctor did the unusual: he came to my home. The next
day, fevered, babbling, and incoherent, I was admitted to the
Century City Hospital, brought in by my daughter when I had
refused the ambulance ordered by the doctor.

In the darkness that enfolded me I did not even know that
I still existed. I did not know that my neck was stiff, that a
spinal tap indicated an increase of pressure associated with
abnormal activity in the brain. Low glucose and high protein

*Robert Jay Lifton and Eric Olson, *Living and Dying* (New York: Praeger, 1974),
p. 121.

in the spinal fluid were indicative of meningitis, and, because that disease is associated with pneumonia, I was also given a chest X ray, which disclosed a calcified node in one lung. (I had had TB of the lungs as a child.) On the basis of this limited knowledge, I was given three different antibiotics, each one as combatant to a particular bacterium. The identifying culture growth—which would be reported six whole weeks later—was begun.

The next day my right pupil was markedly larger than my left one. *Something* was going on with the cranial nerves. On November 2 I was given a brain scan. (This was before the development of the sophisticated EMI scan, which gathers data so thoroughly today.) An EEG (brain-wave test) showed patterns of unusual slowness; my temperature and the level of mentation (the ability to think) varied, up and down. I had lost track of time and meaning; everyone asking, everything asked, received a "Yes." (Was the compulsive yeah-saying, the agreeableness, a way of bargaining for acceptance and help when most functional capacities had disappeared? Later, when I was recuperating, I tried to regain this pattern of behavior. If, as I began to feel then, I had shown my anger, my frustration, or rejection of the situation, I was afraid that I would have alienated the sources of support so badly needed.)

By the fifth of November, the pupils in both eyes were dilated, and I was unresponsive to any voice—medical personnel, family, or friends. Transferred to the hospital at UCLA, I had become a multiple question mark: Did I have a brain abscess, a tumor, fungial meningitis, viral or partially treated bacterial meningitis? Hypothesizing, the medical consultants labored on. My temperature had lowered; the brain waves recorded by repeated EEGs showed an increased slowing. I was fading away, winding down like a clock running out—a resolute, but worn, mechanism. Multiple medications for the possibility of TB and a steroid for the swelling of the brain were administered. The antibiotics gentamicin and streptomycin were injected both by vein and into the spinal fluid. (These were the healers that destroyed my balance as they saved my life.)

On the eighth day of the month I made my first *purposeful* movement—pulling a blanket up over me—and uttered words but without meaning. A week later, still disorganized and disoriented, in my separate space, I was showing inappropriate affect—not *responding* with feelings, but exhibiting them anyway. Largely incomprehensible, I was making up neologisms whenever I spoke; and by the time I left the intensive care unit, a few days later, I was constantly "fabulating" (as the medical records put it)—making up stories with private meanings and no means of communicating to others. As the month ended, as the daily spinal tap and other tests continued, I was beginning to emerge from that closet self, but still thoroughly disorganized. When I opened my eyes, there was no way to receive information: the room spun, and I could not stop it.

What is told here is not an account of blind faith, of expectations that originated in childhood or later and reappeared neatly in a timely manner when needed. This book is about knowledge, not possibility; it is about what *did* happen, in the light of what might have been and usually has been. We need to *know* more than to *believe.* That is why the research of Elisabeth Kübler-Ross on death and dying and of Raymond Moody, Jr. (the physician who reported on the experience of the clinically dead who "returned" to life) has been so engrossing and influential for many readers. To paraphrase William James in *The Varieties of Religious Experience,* it is no more rational to disbelieve out of fear of being wrong than to believe out of the hope of being right.

Expected to die, I did not. But what I experienced was dramatically parallel to the cases described by these scientists: *for an island in time I reached a dimension of being so true, so valid, so healthy, serene, and complete that it was incomparable to any state of consciousness occupied earlier—or since.* Was it a religious experience? Not in the conventional sense, for no God welcomed me, led me, held me. Unlike the saints of the past, no ecstatic tremor engulfed me. But there are few generalizations or summary words that could describe the ineffable awareness of space and unity, light, warmth, and welcome I experienced. Some of its qualities were those that James considered to be characteristics of religious, mystical visions. These were the *ineffability* of the experience and its *noetic* quality: what occurred defied communication or expression in words, and its occurrence was accompanied by a state of knowledge and insight that did not originate solely in the mind. Less usual aspects of mystical visions were *transiency*—the limitations of their endurance—and the sense of *passivity* that the recipient experienced whose will was held in abeyance to a superior power. The more thoroughly I mended, the more conscious I became of the limitations of my ability to choose. I strove against arbitrary rule.

There is a continuing need for openness to the anomalies of human experience, but this openness, this receptivity and acceptance, does not always imply understanding. Science cannot provide proof for these occurrences; their reality and meaning are intensely idiographic and personal. This is a chronicle of extralife encounter, but it is also one of alteration and struggle in the process of reclaiming my niche in life and my human body, distorted and racked, which had nearly abandoned its functions of both containment and facilitation.

In two of his books, Moody* describes three categories of persons he found in his exploration of life after life:

1. those who were resuscitated after having been thought, adjudged, or pronounced clinically dead by their doctors;
2. those who, in the course of severe injury or illness, came very close to physical death;
3. those who told their experiences, as they did, to others who, later, in turn reported them as responsible, if secondhand accounts.

I belong to the second of these categories. However, probably like each of those describing these experiences, I did not share *all* the commonalities many did. I had, for example, no sense of movement within a long, dark tunnel or separation from my physical body, no floating away. Neither the dead whom I loved nor any religious figure nor a theoretical Ideal or Composite (God?) appeared to me. No "Other" came to help me in the transition to another place of existence. And my life was not played back for evaluation and summary.†

Withdrawn, I was not disengaged, as many of the aged become when the end is nearing. In my passivity, I was still in the sweep of continuing social action. Even in the isolation of

---

*Raymond Moody, Jr., *Reflections on Life after Life* (New York: Bantam, 1977) and *Life after Life* (New York: Bantam, 1975).

†Following his own research, Kenneth Ring, a psychologist at the University of Connecticut, has systematized Moody's model of near-death experience. He has found that the core near-death experience unfolds in a characteristic pattern of five stages: (1) peace and contentment; (2) detachment from the body; (3) transition: entering the darkness; (4) experiencing comprehensive, enveloping light; and (5) entering that light and a world in which beauty is vividly experienced and where life review takes place and where dead friends and relatives, as well as godly presences, are encountered. (This experience is so valued that those who return to life may express their resentment at having to leave.) Apparently the earlier stages are most commonly reported; the later ones manifest themselves with systematically decreasing frequency. Fewer people report them.

unconsciousness, removed to an absent world, I felt the presence of attention and caring, the omnipotent pressure of love's focus.

My children—Martha, Garth, and Bethany—with me through night and day in that intensive care unit, were giving me life. I might have been faced not only with the hazards of physical death, but also with those of *social* death—acts chosen by others, a death that involves the removal of the supportive presence or the repetitive contacting of friends and family. Its manifestation is withdrawal. Permanent or temporary, complete or partial, it can cause psychic deterioration or physical death, especially when combined with illness. Even in prolonged unconsciousness, I was never abandoned or treated as if nonalive. The life-believing, vitality-insisting orientation of my visitors demanded my perseverance. (Later, the gradual mitigation of that social support for life was difficult to cope with. I had to relearn patterns of communication, remember to call or write, and, when people were with me in person, to extend myself beyond the tight and narrow cave of my own body and immediate space.)

What did occur to me was an intensity of wholeness, of joy, love, and peace—in radiance and luminosity—which surrounded and penetrated my being and was in no way personified. Can one be prepared—even by reading or hearing the reports of others—for the experience of such radiant and focused warmth? Probably not, simply because it is *unbelievable.* To most modern urban dwellers, it is as unlikely as a fairy tale. Overwhelming, it transcends all categories and eludes description. Its qualities cannot be named, nor can its boundaries. All accounts of mystical experience describe the paradox and its ineffability: a void appears, primordial nothingness pregnant with all existence, containing it all in germinal form. The problem is that what can be described in words is not the object or the action experienced. How can I communicate what is indescribable, convey the power of feeling, the comprehensive joy and sense of completion?

For humans facing biological death, experiences of heaven and hell occur as they do for many psychedelic drug-takers. I did not encounter hell, but my perception of an infinite source of love has made me alter my attitude toward heaven. Some eschatological mythology came to seem possible. In no sense ephemeral, this experience has profoundly altered reality for me. Work, however interesting, is not an end in itself, nor is professional achievement the be-all and end-all of existence; relationships, however stimulating and valued, build permanence through crisis or disappear. I know who I am now and who others are to me. Increasingly, I have come to know that life cannot be fully understood without the recognition and experience of death. Death, as a meaningful, enriching, utilitarian concept, need not be seen as destruction and finality. Accompanied by love—abstract yet personal, invasive yet not intrusive, encompassing without suffocating or obliterating— death becomes an enlargement, an enhancement, of life. Unamuno's tragic sense of life—based on the fear of termination —disappears forever.*

In the middle of December, this powerless puppet, inappropriately euphoric, filled with cheer without cause, went home from the hospital. A container nearly emptied, I did not know the date or even the season, my birthday, where I dwelt, or even what I lived in. I did not know that I had been robbed of my ability to direct my destiny. I could not promise myself or my family and friends that I would not be defeated because

---

*Miguel de Unamuno wrote a powerful and poetic essay, a cry of rage against death, which he called *Sentido trágico de la vida.* This was published in English by Dover in 1954 as *The Tragic Sense of Life.*

I was completely unaware of how little of my vital forces were left still engaged in battle. There was nothing self-conscious about my marginal existence then. Unlike the stroke victims I read about later who were aware very quickly of what had happened to them, I did not know I could not walk or talk nor wonder if I ever would again.

The damage to my body was extensive and real. My functioning was severely limited by the failure of both hearing and vision; I had lost a great range of sound and sight. Without my awareness, my mind had been altered, had become a ruptured variant, easily distracted, incapable of abstract thinking at all or even of sustained effort of any kind. Speech and the processes behind it were misformed and lacking: my talk was the arbitrary substitution of one word for an irretrievable other, each intended to be specific but, in actual practice, vague and complex.

Each day had lost its individuality and its order; each merged with the ones before it and following. Distance in time and space does not cause the ultimate, irremediable separation between people; it is forgetfulness that does that. The forgetter is trapped in an ahistoric discontinuity, alone. This great necessity—human memory—is not a simple repository, not just a storehouse, a library, or a computer core memory—a place where items of information are stored until wanted. It is an intricate, dynamic system that can be made to deliver information about discrete events or items it has had experience with in the past. This information is not fixed but, rather, is continually reorganized as a *consequence* of the processes of interrogation and retrieval. It is highly redundant, so at least partial retention is likely even if the system is grossly disturbed by disease or injury. I did not know what had been retained; I had no sense of loss. I was greatly altered.

Thoughts, the customary whirlpool of ever-arising, ever-lapping images and concepts, were almost gone—the fecund waters now a barren and dessicated plain, their shallow remains evaporating inaccessibly. My once boiling and generative mind was still. I had gone to sleep, as the shamans say, in a nest of ravens and had awakened holding the claw of an eagle.

I was alive, but seriously defective—and, not yet but soon, I realized it.

2

WITHOUT A NAME
OR HISTORY

Recalled from the shades to be a seeing being,
From absence to be on display,
Without a name or history I wake
Between my body and the day . . .

—W. H. AUDEN

Unlike Sylvia Plath, long haunted by death and a once-failed suicide before her final success, I have no call for dying. Some believe that the fear of death can only be assuaged by insisting that life itself is worthless. But I have never thought of life as a death sentence or that humans are mortally stricken with life because that condition always ends in death. Nor do I believe that the passion for self-destruction is a creative one. But the fear of death as "an everlasting nothingness, as if that could be some sort of conscious experience, like being buried alive forever" (as Alan Watts described it), that is destructive, too. It burns holes in present plans, limits attempts, trials, extension. The fact that attempted suicide was once punishable by death is a macabre historical irony.

During my illness I was never afflicted by the presence of death. It was a silent, impalpable, invisible power, barely beyond the senses, accessible and actual to all those around me, but never to me. At the time, I did not believe the accounts of those who were there and saw me labeled and claimed. This in itself was a metamorphosis since, as a child, I had awakened in the night, over and over again, panicked and sweating, trying desperately to free myself from the menacing, encroaching face that advanced overpoweringly in my dreams. Nothingness, then, was not sensationless; it was full of pain and vivid fear, imminent and real.

Was the difference solely a sparing lack of imagination, a saving distance based on ignorance and, later, disbelief? I was not *expecting* death or even illness—and is an act of faith in life that implementory? I do not know. You have to be really alive to mind dying. If you are dying by degrees, as unaware of your predicament as I was, the boundary being slipped over will not even be noticed. It is contempt for life that breeds the death wish. If life is good, why should anyone want to die? And fear of death is rooted in the desire for life's pleasures as well as belief in a negative or vacant afterlife. If I believed my self would be transcended in death, I would not need to fear it. My confrontation with death and its meaning came long after this physical occasion was over. I have come to believe that the *ars moriendi*—the art of dying—includes the practice of alternative approaches to *life,* approaches that have been mediated by the knowledge of death.

I was saved from the fantasies that others concocted about my illness and my proximity to the cliff at the end because the alarms and extremities that the professionals knew to be associated with it were largely kept to themselves. At the time, dying was never a real issue to me; the thought of it never crossed my mind. But, increasingly as I grew better, the fear of mutilation—partial, warped destruction—grew. It came and went, depending on my own self-consciousness and my perception about how others were regarding me.

Illness *is* a figure of speech or a metaphor (as Susan Sontag has pointedly argued).* This is an inescapably personal phenomenon as well as a (perhaps differing) social one. The culturally derived meaning may be demythicized; the individual conception may not. Who could think of these mutilations, these deprivations and shrinkages of ability, as merely the signs of a superior nature? *I* could not. Yet that was the historical stereotype of TB—a becoming frailty as unreal as the one of the typical female who is defined as sweet, docile, and ignorant.

> We betray the past when we forget its disquieting realities; we redeem it in the present when we remember the truth, extend that memory into the future, and apply it to the accomplishment of valued goals.

I found this statement in my papers, written some time ago as a note to myself, still well and not imagining the meaning of a truly lost past. Yes, I had heard of amnesia and believed in it—in a storybook way. Its romantic dimensions were unreal and, therefore, agreeable and curious, for inspection at a distance, preferably a literary or a film one. When I became conscious after my illness, *everything* cognitive was gone—images, concepts, words, and recognition. Not irretrievable (as I believed when my awareness first grew), it was the connec-

*Susan Sontag, *Illness as Metaphor* (New York: Farrar, Straus & Giroux, 1978).

tions, the bridges, tapes, wires, hair threads, microscopic passages between aspects of myself that were coated with layers of impenetrable fixity. They were not absent, only frozen, immobilized in place, awaiting the tutored thaw that would come in time.

I could receive but not identify, feel but not recognize the reason for (or the meaning of) what was felt. I heard noise, but much of it—even speech—was not comprehensible. I was receiving sound separated from thought. Evidence and experience were not accessible. The buildings of my childhood, youth, and prior adulthood were torn down; straight routes became a maze without solution, blocked, their boundaries blank and closed. The inaccessible was not a basket of fruit, breads in a cupboard, available for the taking. All of the past, its sustenance and furnishings, were effectively gone because there was no means of entry into its territory. I had become a disoriented spook.

The old joke that speech is a substitute for both thought and action is untrue. Speech as communication cannot exist without thought and action. Thought gives it meaning; action gives it presence and power. It cannot exist without memory either: non sequiturs bump into each other. The listener must jump from one floating iceberg to another as each disintegrates in turn. My talking was not psittacism—repetitive, meaningless speech—but independent segments unjoined or brought together without obvious relationship.

Just as much of the past—its action and its imagery—was inaccessible without reminders, I had to hear the words that I wanted to use before I could count on their availability. The words were not *consciously* known, but the information I had was not gone; it was simply too far back in the storage cupboard to be reachable. It was not like the experience of aphasia, when the data are available in the mind but cannot be put into speech until each word is repeated.

In the past, the magic of learning, of incorporation, retention, and transfer, had developed for me piece by piece, as it does for everyone. Some of it was planned by the learner; much was not. Later, partly closed to new knowledge by my faulty sense, I was striving for the records of experience, scratching away to find the underlying images until enough appeared to make a pattern and then, suddenly, *Gestalt!* The parts became a whole; reality condensed out of the thickened atmosphere, decipherable and definable, a recognition of what had been learned earlier. Hidden knowledge, it was still there.

Thomas Aquinas wrote long ago that God annihilates nothing. Even death is merely the perishing of a particular individual, but the substance of that person is not gone. *Nothing, then, even in this massive attack, had been amputated, nothing removed or destroyed.* Sooner or later I would find it, use it. (But this I did not believe until later, and I was not entirely right.)

If memory and its reaping harvest were still intact, I could find them again. What incredible joy! In a highly personalized version of the Protestant ethic of hard work, here were the seeds of faith that made endurance possible. Without them, perseverance would have been futile. Why battle when the outcome will be negative?

In her vivid essay on *Illness as Metaphor,* Sontag describes the social myths of illness as psychologically caused by wayward humans whose beliefs that they are getting their just deserts are widely shared. Punitive or sentimental fantasies of mismanaged emotions have long been associated with disease. In the sixteenth century, a happy person was believed immune to the plague, and even today cancer is regarded "with condescension" (as Sontag writes) as the outcome of the loser personality.

Cure is believed to be principally dependent on the individual's sorely tried capacity for self-love.

Long before it was identified as a bacillus, the "morbid swelling" was described by the Latin word *tuberculum*, the diminutive of *tuber* ("bump" or "swelling"). The person with TB was supposed to be "interesting," unlike the ideal candidate for cancer, who was considered dissociated and affectless. Tuberculosis in the lungs, far more prevalent in the nineteenth century than today, was mythologized as the disease of the sensitive and passive, especially those of artistic temperament.* It was a tender weaning from the passions of life, the disease of the "born victim," a particularly appropriate and just punishment. (Remember, for example, the susceptible heroine of *La Traviata.*) When such a disease becomes glamorous, Sontag writes, "health becomes banal, even vulgar." The ill person becomes dangerously romanticized.

Such imagery is literally deadly, and I was doubly fortunate: first, that, without either pain or consciousness, I did not know what was devastating my body; and second, that my internist, unsure of the meaning of the symptoms I was manifesting, called in a neurologist and a TB specialist, who treated me *as if* they knew. I was overdosed and erroneously dosed with the aim of hedging their professional bets on the identity of my attacker. To do less would have subjected me to greater peril. (*After* I was home from the hospital, the telephone rang with the news that the laboratory growth had confirmed some guesses and certain medications could be stopped.) My doctors were faithful to the basic dictum of their education: *primum*

---

*Few people know that TB can appear in many organs: the brain, kidneys, larynx, and the long limb bones, as well as in the lungs.

non nocere—"above all, do no harm." The complexities of sophisticated intuition saved my life. And, because I did not know the meaning of the label *tubercular meningitis,* my ignorance freed me from their expectations.

I remember none of it but the sleepy reawakening, the realization of hustle that was directed at me, the difficulty in standing, the incredible made credible—unimaginable put into imageful practice—with the appearance of the wheelchair, and then my doctor's cautionary words: "It'll be a year or so . . ." (A year or so! What on earth did he mean?) Most fortunately for me, all of my physicians avoided informing me who I was going to have to be, the one-tenth person I had become. They kept their knowledge and their real expectations to themselves: three years at least and then only limited recovery. In vigorous middle age, professional life—perhaps even intellectual life on an amateur basis—might well be over, as the figure skating and the backpacking were, forever. They were avoiding, and with good reason, the demoralizing imposition of their beliefs about duration, sequence, and ultimate outcome.

So when I went home from the hospital, I had no idea of what lay ahead—any more than I missed my past. Nobody lied. They just did not tell me what they knew. They were hoping *for* me, not *with* me.

What had happened while I lay in monitored suspension, buttoned into place, automatically charted and recorded? The UCLA hospital was the Garden of Eden and I, created anew and innocent, a scant and scarce rib of hope. So many people felt the need to participate in the process of my illness. By admitting how much they cared, they sustained themselves as they re-created me. Parent, aunt, sisters, offspring, colleagues, friends—even the estranged partner of an ended intimacy and a former husband, Allan, caring and cooking for the young adults who had once been his stepchildren—all came. One daughter, Marty, flew from Virginia after two days of frantic telephone consultation with a badgered physician in California. ("Yes, she's dying! But I wish the family would stop calling me!" None of my family has gone back to use his services again.)

My son, Garth, drove from Berkeley. He found his observation post in a quiet medical storage closet across from my room. Later, my Aunt Martha described it to me as a very small space with cupboards in the back and with room for only two straight chairs on each side, facing each other. It was the only waiting room for relatives of intensive care patients, and almost everyone who came took a turn there since only two people at a time were allowed to be with me.

My father was dreadfully beset. Informed that I was dying, he had come to say good-by, had left my mother in intensive care at a Tucson hospital where she had just had an elaborate heart operation—a leaking mitral (plastic) valve replaced, a bypass vein from her left leg building aid for the coronary artery pumping blood to muscles. When he kissed me as he left to return to her side, one of my children told him that my head had moved, that I had responded. But, for him, I was already and permanently labeled "Out of Reach." He did not believe her.

(Remember, now: the sick person is a *living* person, not a dead or dying one, right up to that final moment. Do not bid farewell too early; a premature conclusion may be the shove that speeds the parting.)

On his way home to Arizona, this quiet, polite gentleman uncharacteristically fought with an airline attendant over the placement of his cane in the airplane: he needed it by his side; she wanted to remove it to a closet. Only once in our lives, as children, had we seen him slam down a book and swear a single, heart-felt "Damn!," stamping out of the apartment in resentment that he was coming down with the flu.

Unconscious, I was still burdened by the pressure of commitments and productive activity. Over the next year these stories (and many more) were told to me: how, for example, I had surfaced two or three times, once to unplug myself completely and wander through the corridors, looking for someone or something, until my daughter found me. Although I could not see it or tell the time, I had needed my absent watch and demanded it over and over again until it was brought and fastened on my wrist. Like Robert Frost, I still had promises to keep and miles to go—on time—before I slept . . . Or so I must have believed.

One day, they told me, as I lay silent and out of reach, I announced abruptly from my bed, "I *must* get back to work!" This was the first intelligible speech, grasped by the hearers like a beginning shoot of green growth to augur the arriving spring —a spring yet a long way off. I did not speak again for a month.

Throughout the long, repeated night sessions in the intensive care unit, it was my children and two friends of theirs (and mine), not the professional staff, who watched me, guarded and sustained me. Sitting close by the bed, they took turns reading aloud, pouring hours of healing poetry and prose, drama and fiction from Shakespeare and others into the soft night air. The ears of my body were closed to sound, the eyes to sight, but the pores of the soul were open to the drifting presence of warmth and love, submicroscopic and therapeutic. It was, as Saint John of the Cross wrote, that "delicate touch that transforms death into life!"

Later, I came to understand all of the ingredients of those dark and serene hours, the messages and contacts, which filled me within the coma and helped me to emerge with such ineffable contentment. Hell may be others (as Sartre wrote), but so is Heaven. I was not told (the telling would not have been believable and, in any event, was not receivable); I *knew* the power that surrounded and supported me. The manuals on nonverbal communication do not deal with these inexplicable matters.

Part Two

3

PARTICIPATION-
OBSERVATION

. . . what we hear and observe of another person
or an event in which we are even minimally involved, necessarily is influenced by *our* presence.

—THOMAS COTTLE

Coping with illness, death or change in any form can be a
collective enterprise. None of us can remember everything, but
recounting and recording what has happened is a way of holding tightly to that intangible past, of preserving it. I have relied
on subjective accounts and records, both oral and written, to
recover my own past; but where I intrude upon the pasts of
others—those of family members, friends, and colleagues—I
have had difficulty. I know their experience only by report and
consequently feel inauthentic despite my response to it. I cannot live through these remembered times with them, nor can
I identify with the woman they describe even though that
woman was myself. I was not there at the time. I read these
tales only a few steps closer to their reality than you, the
nonparticipant reader.

This I know: I was not only "child-changed"—as Cordelia

called her father—but sister-, parent-, and friend-changed, as well.

Here are Jascha, poet, professor, and friend; Joan, my sister; Allan, an ex-husband who refuses to be alienated; and my oldest child, Marty. They were, and still are, participant-observers, in the sociological use of the term, directly acting and acted upon during the events they observed.

JASCHA KESSLER

In the fall quarter of 1974 I was preparing to go off to Europe, Iran and Israel. Calling you, we learned from one of your daughters that you were deathly ill, in Century City Hospital, as I recall, and about to be moved to UCLA, after a couple of days or so of sinking into deep coma. We were shocked. She told us that you had been found weeping in a parking lot at UC, Irvine, late at night, after a day's teaching, by a guard. You couldn't find your car; you were confused and obviously very ill.

I asked a doctor friend and neighbor to look in and find out what the story was. You were in coma, and the chart was bad. Some sort of massive infection of the frontal lobes, I think he said. They were pumping you with antibiotics, into the spinal column. Prognosis for recovery was exceedingly pessimistic. He said you might recover but probably would only remain vegeta-tive, perhaps at best vegetative, much worse than a stroke victim. I got on the line with a psychic healer, a dear friend, in Oregon, and she asked me for details and arranged, lacking a physical token of yours (clothes, picture) to work through me at regular hours, 10 or 11 PM when I should sit and call up your image in silence and she would try to contact me and "hold you in the light". She works "professionally" at that. The best

I could get, as a mental image—not having seen you—was an image of you that was somewhat corpse-like, influenced, no doubt, by the assessment of you by the doctor-friend. I did that for a week. Then I think I recall that your parents had been summoned. Bad news. And then that your daughter said that in stimulating your foot, or the sole of your foot, there was a flicker—your eyelid, perhaps. All the while, the millions of units of antibiotics were being pumped in daily, through the spinal column. We were unutterably saddened by this state of things. I was to leave about the second week in November. I recall that I was in Bruxelles for Thanksgiving. . . . I determined to pay you a parting visit, parting in every way, because I heard you were out of coma and in intensive care.

I went to UCLA and walked right into the Intensive Care Ward. The nurse was near a console. There were about 8, 10, or a dozen beds in the ward. I asked if Elizabeth Simpson were to be seen. The nurse said, "Yes", and pointed. There you were —all the others being comatose in beds—sitting in a chair at the foot of the bed, a chair with an armrest. I watched you. She said that you were awake but non compos mentis. *A bunch of magazines were on the arm of the chair and your head waggled, unseeing, over them, your hands weak, one in your lap, perhaps, the other doodling a page with your finger, aimlessly. I watched. She said that they gave you the picture mags—Ladies' Home Journal, Glamour, Vogue, etc.—in an attempt to stimulate the brain through the eyes.*

With a tremor, I asked if I could approach you. "Of course," she said, "Any stimulation is to the good." You wouldn't recognize me or speak coherently, she said. I took a deep breath, approached you and, drawing up a chair, knee to knee, I sat with you. I was, to say the least, shocked at your appearance, though not surprised. How many weeks of coma had it been?

Pale, hair matted and colorless, lips murmuring and mumbling nothings, you sat. Eyes quite vacant. Behind you a monitor beepbeeping over your shoulder, lights and oscilloscope with its waves. Tapes to your head, shoulder, and one tape wired to your left wrist. One to your ankle, I think. As if you were a zombie kept going by the electrodes monitored to you. When you lifted your head to stare at me, I said, "Elizabeth?" You didn't know me. I took your chin and kissed your face, cheeks, and forehead. Three kisses? I said, "It's Jasch." Your eyes focussed. A light seemed to come into them. It was a light of recognition. You repeated, "Jasch?" "How are you?", I said. And we began to talk.

I tried to be clear and simple and reassuring, and "normal". I told you that I had come to see you before I went away, that I was taking a trip. And you said, "Oh yes, you're going to New Mexico, to Taos?" Delightedly. "Have a good time!" I was surprised. I realized you were remembering that I had been [scheduled] to go in August. It was as if you'd had electroshock and everything since August was expunged, but the older memory was there and it came right up. (The magazines, I forgot to say, were upside down and you were staring at the upside down pictures vacantly, which had pained me at first and made me feel that it was hopeless.) But the conversation was coherent. I told you where Julie [his wife] had been in the summer, and you nodded, and seemed to be trying to grasp the temporal sequence and facts. I stayed, talking to you, for about ten minutes, perhaps a bit more or less, trying to gauge your strength.

Holding your hands and stroking your head. I felt that the stroking was possibly good for you. I rubbed your head, neck, shoulders and arms, gently, lover-like. You responded, sexually, like a child—a girl of five or six. That was good and right, I felt.

You purred. And so I did all that, crooning the news and so forth to you. But you were there and knew me, and knew what I was saying. "You get well, you be strong, you be all right", I commanded. And you said, "Yes, yes, yes", and so on. I left desolated. The nurse asked me if you had responded. I told her you knew me and knew me as of August, confused about the recent weeks and blank, in fact, puzzled. The nurse was quite surprised. I wished I weren't flying away and commended you to the Powers above, so to speak.

I tell you all this because it may be of interest that in the state of Nothing you were yet there, at some level below the consciousness you have of unconsciousness. It is another marvel of the power of the nervous system, apart from mind, spirit, will, and vegetative health and recuperability. And modern medicine . . . too.

That's all I have for you. It's all quite vivid. Knowing you for a very sensual, sexual person I intuitively worked on that end with you, too—as a friend, a male, and full of health as I was, hoping to give you what are lamely called 'vibes' and aura. As ever, love, Jascha.

September 1978

JOAN SIMPSON BURNS

Dad called late Tuesday afternoon to say Elizabeth was dying and he would have to go, so could I come and stay with Mama (in a manner of speaking, since she was in the hospital). I had just known since Sunday that E. was ill. For some reason I had thought meningitis was polio (Jim [her husband] knew better) and my fear had been that she would be paralyzed. Now he said she was in a coma.

Jim and I arranged my flight to Tucson for the next day. This was election night and we had planned an open house for Jim's students and any members of his department who could come. We expected some seventy people and were going to feed them cider, beer, coffee and doughnuts . . .

I thought I would be all right if I could just stop crying . . .

The children's support was so important to me. My step-daughter, Deborah, left me a note that night: Please have a fruitful trip out west tomorrow. I hope everything turns out all right. *And my daughter, Trienah, wrote to me once I had arrived in Tucson to be with Mama:*

> Pappy [Jim] called this morning to tell me the news. It is very discouraging. It must be lonely for you to be in Tucson as Grandpa and Marty [Aunt Marty, her Grandpa's sister] are both in L. A. and Grandma, I assume, is still in the hospital. Don't let it get you down. It must, though, be easier to feel that you are doing something and not just sitting and waiting; even though you are still waiting. Like you always tell me, keep yourself busy. It's good advice at a time like this. That is what I'm trying to do.
>
> I wrote the Simpson kids a nice long letter and will write to Grandma soon. I assume that by now she is out of intensive care so give her all my love and lots of hugs and kisses from both of us. Tell her we did whatever it is that atheists do; cry, worry and take tranquilizers, I guess. I think I have been particularly worried and sort of susceptible because of not feeling so good . . .

I spent the first few days in Tucson coping with mechanical problems—learning to drive my parents' car, figuring out various routes in a strange city, wrestling with strange door locks, washing machine, dishwasher, new-fangled iron. Outside, the sun was very warm, the air pleasant, but the inside of Mama and Dad's house, while familiar, always seemed cool to me. I watered the gardens, sat with Mama at the hospital but tired her, I'm afraid, as we talked a good deal at first, getting caught up. When I got back from the hospital, I'd get myself supper, read a murder mystery in bed and sleep as if drugged. Like being in limbo . . .

"Little" Marty had gone out to California as soon as news had come that Elizabeth was in the hospital. Apparently, E. had been sick for some weeks before that, with an ear infection and peaking fever, etc., and was not hospitalized until a tentative diagnosis of meningitis was made. I can't help wondering whether she was let go too long. She was put into isolation at first while the doctors attempted unsuccessfully to culture material from the spinal column. She was being treated with massive doses of antibiotics, which were frightening in themselves because of possible side effects, and had, I think, been in a coma three days or so before Dad went out—after the doctors said she was dying.

When Dad kissed E. goodbye the last day before returning to Tucson, the right side of her face was paralyzed and she was still comatose. He thought he was saying goodbye to her for good. But when "Little" Marty picked Dad and Martha up at the motel the next morning to drive them to the airport, she was able to tell them she had just seen her mother and that E. had spoken to her. She was no longer in the coma.

When he got home, Dad was bitter because he hadn't been told that morning that Elizabeth had come out of the coma in time to see her before his flight back to Tucson. His last memory of her was saying goodbye to what he thought was virtually an already dead person, paralyzed and in a coma. He told Mama all of this in the hospital and she listened, sitting up in her bed. "Poor dear, you've had a horrible time!" she said.

I had to get back to High Mowing [the Burns's home in Massachusetts]. I hoped to see Jim for at least a few hours before he left for the west and then, too, someone had to cover the house while he was gone. Mama was coming home from the hospital on Monday and Helen [Joan and Elizabeth's older sister] was arriving in Tucson that same day to be with them for a few days before returning to Rochester from Los Angeles. So I arranged to give her the car at the airport (along with Martha for a guide) and fly off to Los Angeles the next flight after that. I felt I must make that trip then—that I could not go all the way back to Massachusetts and then fly out again for a funeral but, most of all, I wanted to see Elizabeth while she was still alive, although we were by then becoming more optimistic. She had survived the coma and the enormous doses of antibiotics to emerge, at least for the time being, without paralysis and with some eyesight and hearing intact.

I see before me now Elizabeth's face as she lay in her hospital bed, the peculiar shape of it; thin and distinctive, eyes closed, face not pallid but the flesh tone still warm from a tan kept up through the fall. She lifted her lids with great languor, and her eyes did not quite focus although she looked upward to where Marty stood somewhat behind her. It was as if she were incredibly exhausted and could do no more than respond when prodded. She volunteered nothing but her smile.

I told her how beautiful she looked. Indeed, all the beauty in the world seemed concentrated to me in that face by virtue of the fact that she was alive . . . She smiled faintly. I kissed her forehead and told her how dearly I loved her and she smiled *at that, eyes still closed. Her teeth seemed small and perfect when her lips parted as she fell into a light sleep. Marty, nervously stroking her arm, woke her out of that by asking questions, to which she responded with assurance—although not always correctly.*

I wept in the hallway and said to Garth, "I just hate to see her like this", to which he replied, "I know".

An intern came by and tested her reflexes, all of which were good. He addressed her as "Mrs. Simpson"—to which she made no response. Marty and I explained that "Mrs. Simpson" was Elizabeth's mother, that she was "Dr. Simpson". She answered immediately when he addressed her that way. Then he asked her name. She said in faint tones, "Mary Elizabeth Léonie". He looked baffled and we had to explain that that was her name—the first three of them. "Where are you?" "In the American Museum of Natural History." "What are you doing there?" "Talking to you." (This was said in the tone of "What do you think I'm doing!") Marty and I suppressed giggles. "Are you in bed?" "No. (Pause.) I was this morning though, before now."

I checked with the doctor to see whether so much activity was all right and he said it was good for her to be stimulated as much as possible.

As we drove to the apartment, Marty and I agreed we would take up the matter of finances later, in a manner that would permit any of the others to participate if they wanted to do so. We started the conversation around the table after dinner. Bethie had her sewing machine set up in the dining room and was working on a blouse; Marty was embroidering a night shift for her mother. Bethany said the hospital has asked them to pay a $700 bill, what was left over after an 80% payment by Blue Cross Hospital Insurance. I said that idea was to preserve *as much money as possible for E., to help her get back on her feet, that they must figure on at least six months' convalescence.*

Garth said that she'd be out of the hospital in a week or so and would go right back to work. I told him that it was unrealistic to think that way and the only way we could help her was by planning. Then Garth said angrily that I was talking as if she were going to die! "No," I said, "I'm talking as if she's going to live!" He flung himself out of the room, refusing to listen further. "I'm not going to listen to any more of this!"

While we were discussing these things, Marty looked Bethany straight in the eye and asked if it had occurred to her that she might not be able to go to the university at Berkeley next semester. Bethie looked shocked. The next morning I put down on my list: everyone plan to get jobs as soon as possible and pay as much of the rent as you can—the single horrible ongoing expense, except, of course, for E.'s fantastic hospital bills. I agreed that the apartment should not be given up, that E. needed it to come back to, and such a move was to be considered only later when we had a clearer picture as to what was going to happen.

Marty drove me to the hospital that morning, where we saw E. again. The nurse washed her and she responded correctly when she was asked to roll over on her right or left side, gave the correct arm and so forth. On our way out, I gave Marty money for a natural bristle brush for Elizabeth's hair and Marty then drove me to the airport. I was glad she was there and told her so. She was sensible and managing.

The flight back was dreadful. I had only minutes to make my connection in Chicago and the plane stood on the ground in L. A. for some time with the auxiliary electrical system not functioning. We then made up that delay only to circle for some time at Chicago. I had about ten minutes to get my connecting flight, at a different airline, which meant I had to go into the terminal some distance. I ran, puffing like a whale as I carried my heavy hand luggage, and then collapsed into my seat. The stewardess very kindly put my bag up front in a compartment. The weather from Chicago to Albany was awful and the plane bounced so much I though I would lose what food the previous airline had fed me. I was exhausted by the time we·put down, walked in a sort of daze into the building and then realized I'd left my suitcase on the airplane. I ran back and got to the door we'd entered the terminal through just as it was being locked and the man walking away. I banged on the door to no avail. A group of employees nearby watched me. One told me to go to the airline's counter. I walked rapidly down the hall, weeping into my kleenex, trying to hold it over my face. At the counter, the airplane was called and the stewardess and pilots brought my bag off, everybody looking at me with some question because I was crying so hard . . . When Jim came back from California, I wrote my father:

> *Jim's report on Elizabeth is somewhat promising. He estimates that the chances now range from her being able to take care of herself physically and live a perfectly pleasant life, perhaps with one of the children living with her, to her being able to resume intellectual activity. If that last happens, he believes it will not be for some time. But I believe the person we knew as Elizabeth is there, which is something to be very grateful for. She was not out of intensive care when he saw her but was to be moved the following day. The nurse reported that she was still having comatose periods but while Jim was there she was alert, sitting up in bed and taking regular food, and carrying on a discussion with him about her educational philosophy that seemed to him perfectly sensible. When asked what she taught, however, she said, "English"—which she had in the past, but some time ago,*

*in a high school. She made odd connections—something like
"The students are greatly concerned with . . . potatoes." He
didn't test to see whether she remembered or recognized him
but thinks she may have called him back to her bedside by name
after he spoke with the nurse. When he kissed her, she said,
"That feels nice."*

*All this is much different from when I saw her and encouraging
—but scary in some ways.*

*There is no prognosis but things look hopeful as long as she
continues to improve, which she certainly has been doing. She
has taken to reading aloud the cards, etc., she gets, to everyone's
surprise. She handles liquids well, feeds herself somewhat clum-
sily but is improving at that. She seems comfortable, Marty says,
but is starting to say that she's confused. Marty said the same
thing that Jim did about her starting sentences sensibly and
then ending them nonsensically.*

*The bill over and above Blue Cross is now coming to around
$1,000 every two weeks, but this should go down somewhat now
that she is out of intensive care and with the children acting as
her special duty nurses. I suggested that her life insurance
policies be checked to see whether the premiums are suspended
during disability. The staff at Irvine has been teaching her
classes and so her salary will be sent until the end of the quarter.
Marty says that means two more monthly payments. The Dean
of the law school at UCLA, who is a friend, says those will
pretty surely come in as there is nothing illegal about that.
Marty estimates they can easily handle things financially for at
least three months and maybe longer than that.*

Elizabeth once wrote a piece (to me? for me?) in which she
said our souls mingled, much like the love poems, Sonnets from
the Portuguese, Elizabeth Barrett Browning wrote to her husband. E. and I had a psychological "Siamese-twin" relation-

ship, symbiotic. We generally knew what the other was think-
ing, no doubt because we had more in common with each other
than with anyone else in the world, at least for many years,
having shared our childhoods and finding the other the only
constant element during that period when we were shipped
around from pillar to post—saved, somehow, because to-
gether.*

November 1974

ALLAN ROCK

The fall before you became ill I was in the habit of calling
you every few weeks to keep in touch and one day you said that
you thought you'd picked up virus pneumonia, but had not
seen a doctor as you were much too busy. That was a Wednes-
day or Thursday because, on Friday—as Bill and I were loading
the car for a weekend in Carmel—Bethany called to say that
you were in Century City Hospital after going delirious the
night before. I called her daily from Carmel over that weekend
and after returning home on Sunday night. Albeit on edge, she
seemed strong and was holding up extremely well, particularly
considering that she was the only one with you, caring up close
and also communicating with your family all over.

I'm hazy as to the first mention of meningitis—Beth may
have mentioned it as a suspicion over the weekend. When she
told me that you were in coma, either Sunday or Monday
night, it had, by then, been tentatively diagnosed as such, cause
unknown. The next night, when she painted a deadly picture
of your condition, she was very shaky and, I felt, pushing to the
end of her string. Primarily to support her, as I couldn't do

---

*As children, during our parents' prolonged divorce, Joan and I were in the custody
of many different adults in many different places.

much to help you, I told her that I'd be down the next morning. The delay, pure and simple, was for me to get to my deposit box for your will and funeral instructions; she had given me such a bleak picture that I thought it advisable. Flying down the next morning, I rented a car and went straight to the hospital where I met Beth and Lynn [Bethany's close friend] at the Intensive Care Unit. Marty was already there. Although I didn't see either one until later that day, I was told that your father and his sister, Martha, were in town.

Dearie, you were a scary mess! Aside from a generally corpse-like look, I have a vivid recollection of the facts: the muscle structure had completely relaxed and gravity was pulling all of your features down to the resting side. (Oi vey! the man said . . .) With the three girls and Garth who pulled in that afternoon, we took turns holding your hands and talking to you.

Your father came to the hospital later that afternoon, looked in on you briefly and stayed in the hall. Aside from one short talk with Dr. Lewis or Winters, I don't remember him talking to anyone, just standing and gazing. Aunt Martha was with him then. Marty picked up Helen [my oldest sister] at the airport the next morning. An amusing side note: Marty had stopped the car briefly at the apartment where we were getting ready to go visit you, leaving Helen sitting inside it. I answered the doorbell to find a matronly-type looking for an apartment number other than yours, told her that this wasn't it and closed the door. A few minutes later, Marty answered a second doorbell and found Helen there again! Embarrassing, but do recall that I had never seen her before . . .

We went off to the hospital in the two cars and stayed all day, taking turns being with you and sipping coffee in the cafeteria. Winters came through and Helen [who is a biologist] bounced a batch of technical questions off him. Bethany had tickets to a play that night and was going to give them to a friend. I told her to stop feeling guilty about taking a break and to get her ass off to the theater—which she did.

Then you started to show very subtle signs of improvement. We were convinced that your facial muscles were regaining their control. You uttered a few noises at first and then a few simple words. I recall at one point that you made as if brushing something off my arms and giggled, "Butterflies!" as if it were a secret joke. The nurses were always putting physical tests to you—reflexes, that sort of thing—and finally took to asking you questions. One of them asked what you worked at and you told her that you were a school teacher which bothered the poor woman (who knew better). I suggested that she ask you your age and you said, "Thirty"—so there you were, very consistent but teaching high school in Whittier in your head.

I think that your father and Martha went home a bit before I did. Helen was going on to Tucson to see Anne [my mother in the hospital there]. I'm not sure that she was still in Santa Monica when I had to leave on Sunday. The kids had fallen in love with her since she walked into your apartment and put her sleeping bag down. She had the air of simply helping without intruding on their lives. The first day that she was there, she told me of temporary cash problems that she had when Wolf [her husband] was killed in Antarctica: all bank accounts were frozen until the will was probated. The topic implied so much that she left it up to me to suggest that Beth take the money out of your joint checking account and open one in just her own name. Beth was intimidated by the idea of questions from other people about this procedure, so I wrote a check on my account and she wrote one to me for the same amount. Fortunately, it proved to be a wasted effort . . .

When I left Sunday, you were still in the ICU but obviously on the mend. I stayed in daily touch on the phone, even calling Marty at your bedside and, to my surprise, her putting you on *the line. It wasn't a scintillating conversation; I had the impression that you just couldn't form the words to bring out what you had in mind, but it sure sounded good just hearing you try to talk. And so we stayed in touch.*

I came down for a weekend after you returned to the apartment, putting up in an oceanside motel. You were then carrying on about your apartments and the city where you lived. Beth was having none of that; she continually challenged you to name that city, which, of course, you couldn't do. That didn't stop you from bringing it up again a few moments later. You were in a wheelchair and we took you to the Palisades [a sidewalked park a block away that overlooks the ocean]. I think that you may have been just starting to use the metal walker then, too. That was the time when a little ole lady clucked about you "pore, little thing" and how did it happen? and you giggled and said, "Ice skating". When she had gone, you laughed again and commented to me, "That's not what happened, is it?" When Bill and I came down for the wedding, you were still using the wheelchair to get to the park, but were getting better with the walker.

Above all, I remember the children doing everything that had to be done with no nonsense and no fighting and just plain doing everything that anybody could imagine being necessary (or even desirable).

July 1978

MARTY KORWIN-PAWLOWSKI

[A duplicated letter sent to all family members]

Mama is stable, knows her right hand from her left, moves her whole body when asked to and also when not asked to, e.g., for her own comfort, and can drink by herself. She feeds herself but has some problems, possibly the result of very poor depth perception. She recognizes her children from across the room, knows her name, address (street, city and state), phone number and birth date. She says that she feels "a little vague", is a little confused and is "learning". She is comfortable, generally, and very responsive, lighting up in big smiles whenever anyone enters the room.

She has been sitting up in a chair a little bit and seems to like it. At noon today she was moved out of Intensive Care and into a room with only two beds, where it is quieter and much less hectic. We have been doing her special duty nursing—the doctors felt that it really is a plus for her to be with family and people familiar to her—and by now we are fairly experienced anyway!

Her medical status is frankly this: her chances of survival have gone from nothing to something . . . a big jump but her chances are not very good, just a lot better than zero. They still do not know for sure what she has. The choice is of 1) tubercular meningitis (the favorite choice by far. The doctors seem quite agreed that this is most likely.); 2) a fungus infection (She's not being treated for this, since the treatment itself can kill.); or 3) a carcinoma which would, of course, be untreatable and lead to death. A fourth possibility, outruled earlier, is being searched for on Monday, when she will have another angiogram. They will be looking for an abscess, but do not expect to find one. The earlier brain scan showed no signs; this is just to make sure. An abscess actually would be good news, since it would be treatable. If one does not show up, they will begin cutting back on the antibiotics, but continue with anti-TB therapy. They consider that the likelihood of a carcinoma isn't very good. They can find no trace, and there are no tumors present. But apparently they might not be able to find a trace without doing a brain biopsy and maybe not even with one. In any case, no one wants to risk doing that!

Obviously, she is not out of physical danger. In addition to the above, she continues to run the risk of losing her hearing and the possibility of permanent kidney damage. Continuation of the antibiotics can lead to bacterial or fungial problems itself.

As far as the mental state goes, it is apparently impossible to predict recovery. All that is known is that she has generalized brain damage, but no obvious major damage in any specific area. She could get no better, get a little better but not recover fully, or recover fully—any of a thousand possibilities. As of today, she is progressing slowly, but definitely. Nothing can be done now but waiting and helping her orientation process along. Recovery, if it comes, will be a very long and slow process.

It's quite clear that she recognizes her children, and she will give their names if asked. She no longer identifies me as Joan Simpson and hasn't for days and she seems to tell Bethany and me apart now, although we weren't sure at first that she was doing so completely. Today I'm going to take a photo album to her that I made up last night of recent pictures of Grandma, Grandpa, Great-Aunt Martha, Aunt Helen, Aunt Joan, and we three children, plus some of Mama herself. That seems like a logical aid . . .

That's just about it, I think. Just one last note to give a clearer picture of what she seems like now: she responds quite coherently generally to questions like, "Would you like to nap, read a magazine, have a chocolate?" (Usually "Yes!" to that one!) or questions about how comfortable she is. It's possible to have a conversation, though a limited one, with her. Now that she has begun to talk more and more in the vocabulary and terms she is used to working with, she often seems to finish *sentences in sensible ways, but not quite as it seems she may* have meant *to! Here are some interesting statements: for instance, she said the other day, "All households should be set up so that . . ." (very, very slight pause) "women get tickled." Or, on another occasion, "There are many fundamental characteristics . . . of feet." She is beginning to get back into moral development* a little: "Everyone should have morals." And so on. When she reads aloud, and cannot read a word clearly, she either substitutes one which looks like the difficult one or one which (more or less) makes sense in the sentence.*

She is on a regular diet and feeds herself, but she is much better at drinking from glasses than at eating at this point. But she eats rather neatly and more quickly and better at each meal. And quite frankly (I hope she'll pardon the indelicacy), she's eating like a horse! Someone tried to take her lunch away when she was being transferred to the new room and she all but climbed out of bed in reaching for it! She has no paralysis problems anywhere, including that slack right side of the face which has not returned.

If anyone would like to write to her, it would be a good idea to either type or print clearly, and to keep the note pretty short. She keeps asking about mail, and although she has piles of it from her students, they are mostly hand-written and most give her some trouble because of that. It would probably help a great deal if you could put orienting-type information into your notes, too—things like "here in Tucson . . .", "Now that's it's becoming winter in Williamstown . . ." "Now that my sons, Ethan and Ephraim, are off at school . . ." and so on. Reminders of specific, familiar things are thought to be very helpful,

---

*In my professional life prior to my illness, I had been writing and teaching about theories of moral development.

*as well as those which will remind her of things as they are
now: where each person is living and what each is doing and
so forth. If that can be done naturally and comfortably, she will
not only receive the pleasure of reading your notes, but also it
will provide her with input other than that [which] we alone
can provide. We can tell her that Helen Vishniac and Joan
Burns are her sisters, of course, but if she receives notes signed
"Your sister, Helen" or "Joan", then she's getting a different
sort of aid and identification.*

*Garth reminds me that Mama put in a request for
"deep burgundy wine-colored flowers . . . sweet smelling"
and if someone follows up on this not-too-subtle hint of hers,
it would be lovely. (There are signs that she's on the
mend!)*

[On the same day in November of 1974, Marty was more
candid in writing to her lover, soon-to-be-husband whom she
had left behind going to medical school at the University of
Virginia.]

*We have been at the hospital "being incoherent with Eliza-
beth" as Lynn says. It's great to hear her talk and great to hear
her giggle and make these pronouncements, but it's very hard
to tell if she is being cute deliberately . . . The closer she gets
to normalcy, the more terrified I get that she will stop some-
where short of all the way there, and I'm torn between being
with her all the time, which I like best, or not being there so
much because she's so close to normal that it's painful. She's
not really close at all, but she's so obviously in there that she
seems incredibly close . . . I guess it's pretty clear that, even
if a miracle happened, I couldn't come back before Christmas.
I think I may not be able to leave for six months. It's kind of
horrible, isn't it!*

[And then she wrote notes to her mother, to invite her to read and respond.]

Good morning, Mama. I thought you might like to read a note this morning . . . reading offers at least a little variety!

You've been sick for only about three weeks, although it probably seems like it's been longer. You are doing very well, though, and yesterday the doctors took the intravenous feeding away, so that now you are getting your nutrients through your meals instead of directly into your blood stream.

After breakfast today, you might enjoy doing some exercises. One of your nurses suggested that exercises are a very good idea for you to help keep your muscles in tone, and she suggested some good ones for you to do, like wiggling your toes . . . and so on.

Today the toes . . . tomorrow the world!

. . .

Hello Elizabeth Léonie Simpson! This is a report on the status of your apartment. You will recall that your address is 850 Second Street in Santa Monica, California. Your room-mates, a little rat named Bethany and a chubby cat who is peculiar, have been keeping the place up while you are recuperating at the hospital. That is to say, as usual the cat knocks the garbage can over and Bethany picks it up.

. . .

You are Elizabeth Léonie Simpson. Your address is 850 Second Street in Santa Monica, California. You live in apartment 301 with a little rat, your daughter Bethany, and a fat cat, who is slightly peculiar. Bethany is a student at UCLA, and her cat is simply useless.

Bethany is interested in Women's Studies, whereas her cat is interested in being naughty. You will be happy to know that, while you are in the hospital, Bethany's cat is running your apartment. The cat has assumed such tasks as knocking over the trash can, running wildly all over the place (including up the walls), and licking the margarine off with his tongue. He's a big help!

Tatusi the Tum [an Eskimo statue] remains unperturbed throughout all of this. He is still on the little mosaic table next to the big green velvet chair. Next to him is a five-month supply of Psychology Today and, when the pussy cat is behaving, he often curls up in the big green chair to sleep.

. . .

Today is December 2, 1974. You are at UCLA Hospital, surrounded by plants and two slightly batty daughters.

Bethany is formulating policy regarding Women's Struggles while I write these enlightening epistles for you.

Once these vital tasks are well under way, Bethany and I shall attack the problem of preparing for Christmas and for your birthday which will occur on December 20, 1974. You will be 46 years old, and we will have a doozie of a celebration!

Part Three

4

NOTHINGNESS

I woke up at night and my language was gone;
no sign of language, no writing, no alphabet
nor symbol nor word in any tongue—
and raw was my fear—like the terror perhaps
of a man flying from a treetop far above the ground,
a shipwrecked person on a tide engulfed bank,
a pilot whose parachute would not open
or the fear of a stone in a bottomless pit
and the fright was unvoiced, unlettered, unuttered,
and inarticulate (O how inarticulate!)
and I was alone in the dark,
a non-I in the all-pervading gloom
with no grasp, no leaning point,
everything stripped of everything
and the sound was speechless and voiceless
and I was nought and nothing,
without even a gibbet to hang onto,
without a single peg to hang onto,
and I no longer knew who or what I was
and I was no more.

        —AMIR

Nothing is conceptually impossible.
   —NORMAN COUSINS

The entire first year of recovery was like a train ride along the
southern coast of France—the closed and separating tunnels
alternating with the open, unifying views of the seas—finite

limitations and infinite, enlarging possibilities. The limitations were real. Historically, TB has been regarded as an ambivalent metaphor—as both a scourge and as the spiritualization of consciousness. But this romantic view that illness develops an ethereal awareness is oversimplified. What it brings to consciousness may be very different from what is experienced in health; what escapes may be what is no longer important, or it may be the straightforward, crippling effects of physiological change. The disease eats up the person, exposing either the structural core or its absence.

For me, what occurred was not a psychic numbing—a responsive, partial form of death protecting the recipient from a chaotic or painful reality. Nor was it fear—which someone has called "the mother of all the misfortunes of humans." I had no expectation of pain or death, no experience comparable to that of accident victims. It was *emptiness*—a blanking out and stillness of what Isaiah described as the "vacilating flame" of life. There was a blatant, intense confrontation in that absence: no motion, tension, contact, sound, sight, tasting, touch. NOTHING. The interior décor of the mind, conscious or unconscious, was gone in a *reductio ad absurdum* of the functions that define humanity.

Earlier I wrote that "I was concerned about nothing." That was a literal statement, not an avoidance or an exaggeration. As Robert Kastenbaum wrote, "We know little about nothing, and much prefer to convert nothing into anything."* Not my gross physical limitations, but *nothing*—the nonstate, nobeing, no-thing—was the deep source of my problem. I lived

---

*Robert Kastenbaum, "Is Death a Life Crisis? On the Confrontation with Death in Theory and Practice," in *Life-Span Developmental Psychology: Normative Life Crises*, ed. N. Datan and L. Ginsberg (New York: Academic Press, 1975), p. 33.

with an incessant experience of brink and abyss. Its expansive void swept, boundless, to infinity. The landscape of my mind —its tappable, minable, harvestable recources—had been devastated in a comprehensive clearing. Fuels beyond reach, the power stations operated marginally, erratically, with no apparent storage available for the future. Disaster of inner flood, wind, fire, and earthquake had cleared away the potential of what had been destined to come, as if its possibility had never existed or it had already been and gone, forgotten. Promises had been reneged on and expectations voided. In each moment an *isolated* eternity was imbedded.

Trapped in the here and now of space, emptiness, range, openness, an infinitely receding horizon, the endless explorers within my mind went out, began their searches, and abandoned them, lost in razed cities of confused and inaccessible methods and content. The rooting beds of the planes of the mind were infertile. There were no rough surfaces to which wind-carried seeds of thought could adhere, no supportive structures where landed craft could be anchored in safety and their flights coordinated by a central control. Every venture, every concept or image, was ad hoc—brief, faint, and transient.

That nothingness was an unimaginable paradox. Conceptually impossible (I would not have believed it before it had happened to me), it was nevertheless an experiential reality, perhaps akin to some drug responses. It was wrenched out within me—an inner void, an abyss without pattern, frame, finish, or content. The process of search for language or for images was like suspension from a single thread over the airy, almost empty, infinite canyon, and scouting below. Language is the house of all, hanging over the edge of the abyss. To speak is human. Octavio Paz knew, too, that not to be able to speak, to express oneself in words, was to be *less* than human. In that inchoate state, concepts and words, remotely scattered, were accessible by random grabbing, playing frightening blindfold games in a floating vegetable patch devastated by drought. Comprehensive death had no reality to me, but this void within me did. It was an end of being, an end of joy *and* suffering; it was *nonexistence* experienced as I had never encountered death. In nothingness there is no will, no choice. *All* is gone. Perhaps even suffering might have been preferable: if I had hurt, I would have known that I was still alive, still thinking and feeling.

Alan Watts wrote,

> Imagination cannot grasp simple nothingness and therefore must fill the void with fantasies, as in experiments with sensory deprivation where subjects are suspended weightlessly in sound- and light-proof rooms.*

But this fantastic replenishment is an index of life, the filling an act of vitality at work. I have experienced nothingness without this flooding invasion. It was stoppage, solid and still. It was vacancy, vacuity, fixed immobility.

I began with a drowsy surfacing, with a tentative, hesitant, two-dimensional stretch—one way to the universe beyond my self and the other, within, to the warped and shriveled storage rooms with preserves like dried fruit a tenth its size, not empty (as I later feared), but whose richness was inaccessible. In the beginning of my recovery those storage rooms were a vacuum, a void into which only my lack of awareness kept me from slipping. As Cesare Pavese wrote,

*Alan Watts, *The Book: On the Taboo against Knowing Who You Are* (New York: Vintage, 1972), p. 32.

the only way to escape from the abyss is to look at it, measure it, sound its depths and go down into it.

I had found a dimension of existence that was neither death nor the life that I had experienced before. Entering the abyss was unavoidable; I had to *try* to think and to speak, to grope my way to consciousness and communication. Fortunately for me, at that time there were no questions being asked of me and, therefore, no unanswerable ones!

My inability to remember the past, either immediate or distant, had spared me what Edmund Burke, writing his *Reflections on the Revolution in France* in 1790, had named the "living ulcer of a corroding memory." But if, with the simple recollection, the entirety of the experience is *also* gone, living in the here and now becomes a forced, inescapable trap. Either, as Susan Musgrave wrote,

> You are locked
> in a life
> you have chosen
> to remember

or you are caught in the present and bounded. The elements of the past create an eternally new *now*. * If what is significant

*In 1823 Johann Wolfgang von Goethe responded this way when someone toasted memory:

> I admit no memory in your sense of the word, which is only a clumsy way of expressing it. Whatever we come on that is great, beautiful, significant, cannot be recollected. It must from the first be evolved from within us, be made and become a part of us, developed into a new and better self, and so, continuously created in us, live and operate as part of us. There is no Past that we can bring back to us by the longing for it, there is only an eternally new Now that builds and creates itself out of the elements of the Past as the Past withdraws. The true desire to bring the past back to us must always be productive and create something new and something better.

These past elements must not be dwelled upon for the building of the future, but in some way they must be tappable as resources.

cannot be recalled, it must nevertheless somehow evolve within us to develop and produce the present and the future. New meanings are mapped from significant experience, not concocted from imagination. The process of thinking occurring *now* cannot be separated from what has gone *before*. It depends on the learned concepts, images, and procedures. What is left without them is infantile distortion, not mature functioning. "Without the breath of life the human body is a corpse; without thinking the human mind is dead," Hannah Arendt wrote.

Instead of tapping a systematic, orderly, well-labeled file or a computer program already tested and available, I was groping into a ragbag of snards and snatches, bits and pieces, multisized and of varying colors and diverse textures, scraps all accumulated over forty-five years, each stored in a heap from a past occasion, blindly, without marking. I reached in for yardage for a pattern, and out came an odd-sized shred, perhaps what was wanted and, then again, perhaps not. I was building patchworks, incongruent and outwardly unrelated, constructing a larger form in which their differences were given meaning as a part of the whole design. But the patches *were* concepts, they *were* words, and, however inappropriately chosen in the beginning, with practice they began to be more useful, more accurate and applicable. The process was like that of a stiff, impenetrable, new cloth softening with constant washing and use into a properly responsive and absorbent one.

As I became more conscious, I began to realize the dimensions of this abysmal bag. Without being able to control its threads, I gradually became more able to make them commonplace and recognizable. Because I saw change, however infinitesimal, I was not doomed to that emptiness forever. But the search for lost concepts, the groping for words, continued for a long time. In the beginning, words came out like islands, soilless, barren, rocky, lacking life and connectedness. Others' wit and repartee swirled by in winds of interaction, eroding lightly and spinning living meaning over these almost inert wastes.

> I understand a fury in your words
> But not the words.

This response to Othello applied to me as well. It was a fury that, in time, grew out of frustration—the laughable, tantalizing, groping, stretching for words that *could* communicate, *could* express what was meant deliberately and not by accident or at random. I needed to believe in the value of persistence and in hope. All knowledge that does not support this belief is mere sciolism. Had I been capable of imagination, I might have found a brief hegira in fantasy—a flight to a better land —but an empty mind is not a vehicle for traveling.

Did I make sense? Those who heard me read the memory of my past self, unable to understand much that I said or to read my blank mind—literally a *tabula rasa*—and responded with love to the empty three-dimensional form. They re-created me, making me a real person by imaginatively investing that form with the qualities once associated with its physical presence. The family photographs show the reality: the edifice is there but the furnishings, the functionings, the automatic mechanisms are missing. It is form without substance, being without sense.

Somehow, very quickly, I knew it all. Consciousness remained—diluted, truncated, aborted, and dismembered, but still there. I had become a living thing islanded in the present, without past or future, with endless moments of *Now* reaching to the end of the world, an infinity not an arm's length away. Scattered and diffused, I was an incarnation to whom surrender was prohibited: I would not give up.

I began to wonder about the bodily control of Indian yogis, a feat of choice in which the seemingly impossible is made possible by belief. Are they deliberately creating, through their own means, the experience that was involuntarily thrust upon me and rejected? Are they achieving a self-transcendence through meditation when inner sensation, imagery, and thought are absent? Many writers have extolled the virtues of emptiness: one should not be afraid of it, of being drained, for the emergence from confusion to clarity is the actualization of emptiness. Voluntary emptying is described as an act involving the wholeness of things.

> The meaning of emptiness, then, is not that the world is nonexistent or void, but that it is fundamentally open, that it can be interpreted, seen, or related to in many different ways.*

I shared the chaotic initiation to the void reported in this work of Miriam and José Argüelles. But there the correspondence ended.

My emptiness was not a matter of controlled personal choice. Neither was it the nothingness to which the Sufi aspire: a state of void and a zero point at which they could become related to any state of being and achieve "everythingness."† It

---

*Miriam Argüelles and José Argüelles, *The Feminine: Spacious as the Sky* (Boulder, Col.: Shambhala, 1977), p. 100.

†According to A. Reza Arasteh, *Growth to Selfhood: The Sufi Contribution* (Boston: Routledge & Kegan Paul, 1980), the Sufis sought to lose what they currently perceived as labels, knowledge, and concepts, to become empty and attain the state of void. Just as the discovery of zero in mathematics made the system possible, so, too, in the art of rebirth, the discovery of a state of nothingness made final personal integration a possibility. The following is a Sufi tale indicating the importance of achieving *faq'r*— the nothingness in which everything can exist:

A great Oriental court once held a magnificent banquet where everyone was seated according to his rank while awaiting the appearance of the king. At that moment a plain, simply dressed man entered the hall and took a seat above everyone else. His

was the experience of vastness, inactivity, and drought as inflic-
tion—being *smitten.*

Michael Novak has written a moving treatise on nothingness
and its utilization for the reorientation of self within chaotic
society.* His concern is for social effects on the person in
search of meaning, a search provoked by an enduring philosophical crisis. For me, these depths of nothingness—their
dark and reeling formlessness—developed internally as a result
of alien invasion: body before mind interacting with the environment. The experience of the void was physical and comprehensive—space without content. Its emptiness included neither anxiety nor experiential despair. (Not until later did they
occur.) While it was happening, it was an isolated phenomenon without complexity or meaning. I was free neither to
change nor even to understand it, but its enduring record in
my memory, emerging later, was an enlivening sign of potential
for recovery. By the time I was able to know terror, I had begun
to mend; and, as I came to realize what was missing, I could
believe in its retrievability—that the past was not gone but only
walled behind temporarily locked barriers to which, ultimately,
I could find the lost keys. With so much so inaccessible, I, too,
was searching for *creatio ex nihilo,* creation from nothingness.

At first, looking inside or out, I encountered a blank field.

---

boldness angered the prime minister, who demanded that he identify himself and
acknowledge if he were a vizier. The stranger replied that he ranked above a vizier,
and the astonished prime minister then asked if he were a prime minister. Again, the
stranger replied that he was above that position. When asked if he were the king
himself, he answered that he ranked above that, too. "Then you must be the Prophet,"
declared the prime minister, to which the man again asserted that he was above that
position. Angrily, the prime minister shouted, "Are you then God?"

The man calmly replied again. "I am above that, too."

Contemptuously, the prime minister asserted, "There is nothing above God."

In reply the man answered. "Now you know . . . that *nothing* is me."

*Michael Novak, *The Experience of Nothingness* (New York: Harper & Row,
1971).

But then I began to realize that it was no longer completely so, that back there and reachable, touchable, attainable were three-dimensional, complex citied and populated hills with paths already laid out for access. They were there and—I knew it to be so—I could find them. What had come into existence by natural processes had not come out of nothing. What had passed out of my consciousness had not been destroyed; it had not been reduced to nothing. It had only been made inaccessible.

I was transformed only by superficial, not radical, contingency: what ceased to be was not actually annihilated. And when my memory and my intelligence began to return, there was no evidence that it had been regenerated out of nothing —exnihilated. Natural processes do not involve either exnihilation *or* annihilation. What came to be was produced from what already was; it was not newly created. Periods of apparent annihilation followed by reconstruction and redefinition provide an awareness that destruction and disease can be passages of transition rather than termination. Descarte wrote *"Cognito, ergo sum"* and revolutionized philosophy. But the profundity of the saying is spurious. I could not think, but I still *was.* I continued to be—even with an empty, malfunctioning mind —and I knew it.

I did not experience myself watching over the experience of nothingness. The mind's screen was dark, blank, abysmal. No light shone upon it from *any* source; its nonbeing was not even illuminated. Can nonbeing be thought of as perfection, unflawed? There was no sight, no sound, no summons emanating from the void. I was not frightened by it, merely numb. I did not understand it, but I did not need to, then. I was caught in illimitable space, in a sequence not of silence, but of the absence of meaning. My body contained *no* memories—not even ones thirty seconds old—the thoughts that had initiated a remark!

Sometimes opposites define each other. Long after I slowly began to think again and to have access to my conscious mind, I came across a Japanese folk tale that helped me to understand the meaning of the experience of nothingness. It is the story of a great lord's daughter who promised to marry the suitor who could hear the sound made when her fingers struck a drum of silk stretched on a bamboo frame. Many came to listen but none heard. Her father became impatient. Then one day a richly appareled young man appeared from beyond the seas, the mountain, and the valleys. When he was asked why he had come, he replied, "For your daughter!" And when the great lord told him that she was for him who could hear the silk drum and she struck the silk, he said, "I have heard its silence." Then the daughter smiled and laid aside the drum to marry him. Because I have access to the void, I have learned what lies behind it. The abyss was a paradox—an empty, sheltering entryway. Out of its silence has come meaningful sound.

Much later, when the abyss was shrinking and becoming inhabitable once more, I wrote in a still unsteady hand: "Valued existence does not depend upon words or access to concepts." Knowing I lied, I added, ". . . except for humans." *Cogito ergo humana sum:* "And if I could not think, what was I then?" Like Theodore Roethke, I had been one who dared

> to live
> Who stops being a bird yet beats his wings
> Against the immense immeasurable emptiness of things.

5

A SHIFT IN IDENTITY

For eternally and always there is only now,
one and the same now; the present is the
only thing that has no end.

—Schrödinger

On the first day of the new year, two weeks after I had returned
from the hospital, my oldest child, Marty, was married. Her
medical-student suitor, John, had flown in from the University
of Virginia, and a small group of us gathered in my Santa
Monica apartment as Rabbi Cutter—friend and colleague—
united them in a simple, nonsectarian ceremony. The two of
them had deepened and personalized its meaning by writing
a part of it themselves.

I remember the weight of that day and its joy. It held the
formal legitimization of an ongoing relationship already well
established and valued. Caught in a series of informal photographs, the occasion and my *physical* presence, too, were recorded. But how lacking in entirety these pictures of me are!
"Absent in body but not in spirit," we used to write when we
wanted to share an occasion and were prevented by distance.
These photographs present the opposite: the flesh (such as it
was) is there; the spirit or essence of the subject is lacking. They

72

enduringly, remarkably, show the vacancies then hollowing my body and mind, the glazed and absent, distanced eyes still dwelling in another remote, removed land. For me, as for *Macbeth*, my face was "as a book where men/May read strange matters." It was the exposure of an ostensibly secret code, elaborate and private, formally unknown, but, in fact, understood by all who saw. This filmed record of loss is vivid, unarguable, objective. (Today I am intact once more, and snapshots please me: the whole person has returned to occupancy.)

With our deep interconnections we contain each other's lives and deaths in our own minds. Today I can remember my sister Gaylord's death. She had been born with a congenital defect—an enormous hole in her heart—and lived to be thirty, propelled by this heart pumping blood ceaselessly returning, out of place, because the natural barriers were absent. Her life was a daily, even a momentary, miracle, and prolonged expectations of her death were massively weakened by disbelief fostered by the unreality of the situation. She was alive every moment, even blue and panting in illness. I played with her, fought with her as an adolescent, as if we would both live forever, and I finally realized her absence only when her husband, bending over the coffin to kiss her, lifted the stiff, deserted arm in his farewell embrace. The rich tapestry of my expectations for her was abruptly ripped.

During the next few months after the wedding, while John returned to school in the East until he could transfer to the University of California at Los Angeles, Marty and I exchanged roles. My twenty-four year old became the "mother" and her biological parent, a most incompetent but developing "offspring." Responsible, guiding, protective, facilitating, she "raised" me to increase my skills while relying on the security of her presence, her services, and her concern. By then, Garth was in the North again and Bethany convinced that I would find my own way, if that were possible.

The telephone rang again and again that first month home, the callers trying to revive the traces of a social world that no longer existed. Once it was my tennis partner in our adult class, wishing me a rapid return to the courts. She did not know, and I did not tell her, that no such return was possible, nor would it ever be. I took the felicitous wish, not recognizing her voice or remembering our playing together. Colleagues called, their unidentifiable warmth accumulating around me protectively. One, in Cambridge, evoked a garbled reply and abruptly hung up. A peculiarly dented and damaged reality, I was nevertheless continuing to be. That was all he had wanted to know. Undaunted, he flew West.

A clinical psychologist, he brought with him not only his professional skills, but also immediately applicable personal ones. Within a few hours of arrival he had already surmised and summed my psychic state as well as my physical one and, sensing the dark void overwhelming me, systematically provided light and tools to scale its vast spaces and decipher its obscure (but not blank) walls. With sensitivity and persistence, he recounted the details of our connections: where we had met (at a conference) and when, what we knew of each other's work, family, and friends. Together, in that invisible past, we had driven to High Mowing, my sister's home in Massachusetts where she and her husband, Jim Burns, live. And when he reminded me of that trip, the synapses began to be jumped: I remembered, I *remembered!*

For the time he stayed in the West (about two weeks?), I believe that I saw him every day—talking, eating, and driving up and down the curved expanse of ocean highway together. Seated beside him as he drove, I slept and wakened, dozed off and re-emerged over and over again. The tangible warmth of the sun, waters solid enough to walk on stretching to eternity,

fluid vibrations from the car encasing us, his palpable presence
—these were the growing factors, the facilitation, for my barely
emergent self. I accepted him matter-of-factly—like each
dawn, breath, bit of food, or swallow—as the gift that he was.
Later, filled with wonder, I asked myself why he had come all
that way to be with this marginally vital friend. Was it an
expression of the deep concern he had for anyone in "trouble"?
Was he merely curious about the realm of my deterioration?
Had we been lovers, and was this closeness and this support the
outgrowth of that shared time? Accepting, I have never asked.

(A year later I met another male friend for the first time
since my illness. He was presumptive, and I did not remember
any intimacy with him either. "Tell me," I asked him, wondering. "Were we lovers?" He nodded his head, but I did not
believe him. There was an enduring space between us.)

We were all in a quiet panic about money then (or, rather,
my *family* was, since I was concerned about nothing). None of
us—including me—knew what resources I had or what I could
count on continuing by themselves without any active professional involvement. Nothing changed for Gar (who was already
self-supporting), but, at this time, his two sisters assumed the
full burden of providing for themselves, going to school part-
time or—briefly—not at all, while they worked. (John's parents
were putting him through his medical training but, of course,
were in no way responsible for his new wife.)

By the time I was able to think about my finances, or to be
consulted about them, what had looked like the most immediate and insoluble problem—my hospital bill—had been re-
solved. Over and above my medical insurance, it had come to
an unbelievable, unrealizable, *ten thousand* dollars. Jobless and
maimed, how could I ever have repaid such a debt? I could not
have, but my aging, retired, and generous parents could and
did. They did this, believing—for what must have been some

sorrowful months—that the payment would be a real sacrifice, that it would curtail the air and land travels, the voyages that had so enhanced their lives but, particularly, their recent years. This deprivation turned out not to be necessary, and I was as pleased as they were about it. Yes, I needed help and was resoundingly grateful to have it given, but I did *not* want the guilt that accompanied knowledge of its cost to them. When their travels resumed, I was freed, not from gratitude but from a sense of punishing obligation.

Like many other positive aspects of this comprehensive disaster, my good fortune in being the daughter of resourceful and giving parents seemed inexplicable, almost miraculous, to me.

There is an extended temporal trajectory before (as well as after) what is labeled the "moment" of death. Before the event, the waiting involves dying persons in a phenomenological state of suspension. As my son-in-law has described their presence, they are, at this time, already gone, already distinct and separate, no longer really there. Phenomenological death may occur in more limited ways as well—for example, through the loss of a partial self or role function. What may be an orderly and expected progression in aging life is experienced abruptly—as an outcome of survival of illness or, in the case of athletes, simply as the end of a physical function. The weight of its importance to the individual gives it the meaning of death, a sometimes limited and sometimes more comprehensive significance.

Lack of belief staved off phenomenological death and disability for me. By denying its possibility, I produced an effective avoidance of the truth, chalking up each centimeter of progress as evidence that return to total capacity was more than *possible,* that it was *inevitable.* At last I can accept that my figure skating is over, solo bicycling, too, and the irregular, textured trails of wilderness beyond my capacities. I am stuck with the endlessly wobbling walk and disorientation after dark, but acceptance too early might have incapacitated me much further than I am now. Intellectual changes are more difficult to cope with than are physical ones.

The passage between illness and acceptance of its consequences was not simple. Even though I had left the world of the whole, as Violet Wiengarten wrote in her dismay over her illness,* I had to believe that my brain could be reawakened, that my defects were transient. Not long after I returned home from the hospital, I began to be absorbed by depression. Although it was not complicated by feelings of guilt and unworthiness, its underlying accompaniment was the sense of *victimization*. I felt that, for manifestly arbitrary reasons, I was being picked on and abused. And, because the outcome was also arbitrary and random, escape routes from disaster were blocked. I had been chosen for this unacceptable, undesirable attention and I did *not* want it!

Toward the end of my first year of recovery I wrote to my parents:

> Here I am, caught with much in process but out of reach and either hanging, drying by itself in the inert and neutral sun untouched by critical eye or aspiring hand or tackled with tears and frustration and the sense that my small talents are gone forever—just as I was beginning to find some human, meaningful, cohesive way to put myself and my experience, my hopes and my wants to some useful work.
>
> How good of the doctor to write you that he believes I will fully recover (in three or four years, he tells me) and how good of you to repeat it to me! How I need that faith! I am so useless

*A novelist, she kept a moving journal of her fatal illness: *Intimations of Mortality* (New York: Knopf, 1978).

and so lonely. I know it sounds foolish when I also *know* that I am loved. My dear children, sisters, parents, friends. . . . But somehow right now I am an odd thread which has blown, loosely, across the interwoven matrices of others' lives, touching and even being caught into the weave for an instant or two, but not patterned, supportive, indispensable in any way. It seems to be a function of the sickness that I feel so incompetent, useless, and alone—afraid to try. (And this in spite of the fact that last month, for the first time since my illness, I was able to run two hundred steps in place—well, not really in place, but without falling over!)

Since I had regained consciousness, my feelings had been subdued and neutralized; as my mending began to accelerate, these negative emotions became forceful and dominant. I became mired in self-hating sabotage—rationalizing to make wishes and hopes appear to be facts, even trying to locate some spurious good within this evil. I remember Freud's belief that much is won if we succeed in transforming hysterical misery into common unhappiness. But hysterical misery, even as self-contrived drama, has a sustaining urgency to it. Common unhappiness is a *bore*. It is common only in the sense of frequency, for it is certainly not shared. (And if it were, it would probably disappear.)

I felt no longer sweetly abraded by pounding love but, bitten and shaped, had become aware of my impotence, aware, too, that I was contained, as well as buttressed, by these amicable supports. Solid I remained, an unresolvable block, necessarily the dependent, wounded respondent to foci beyond me. I had not realized (and I did not then, either) how much memory is a *social* necessity as well as a pleasure, how much of what is retained in common from the past constitutes the sharing that unites separate lives. There is the loneliness of despair that cannot be shared—a desolation that requires impersonality, separation, and distance—epoche—to engender and nuture the re-creation needed. Solitary, distant, and apart, I had become anonymous.

Life becomes most immediate when it forces the individual into a corner. But I must know or at least intuit what corner I am in! I must believe in my own capacities in order to respond to that force! The need, the trick—and it *is* a learned trick—is the transformation of wounds and crippling into performance. As Leonard Kriegel, himself a polio cripple from childhood, wrote, "Disease claims a territory, embeds itself in the mind's geography."

A time of deep depression came for me. No visual configurations, symbols of death, or death words sprang up within me, but I was sensitizing myself, preparing—barely escaping a sense of expectation and, yes, even anticipation. Death was becoming a most subtle stimulus; life, a dirty vaccum sucking me noisily into blank depths. Death was becoming my adviser, but not in the positive, motivational way described by Carlos Casteneda. I could not have left the coma to die; life forces were pulling at me too strongly. Could I lay me down later with a good will and will myself to go?

I could not remember having felt this way before. Even if I had, I was not going to endure this pain—not forever more, no, not even now! I would not have it. One must squeeze the victim out of oneself, drop by drop. Choose for vigor; opt for life! Even in depression, I was stubborn, like my Grandma Simpson, about whom I had published a poem some years before. It was called "The Argument" and went like this:

> My grandmother, apostate,
> Jumped from the Presbyterians
> (But not in Arkansas

Where they shoot them
And stuff them for trophies)
To the Unitarians, belonged
To the D. A. R. by
Way of Honolulu, Tierra del Fuego,
And the Sign of the Cross;
Today might have been
A doctor. She was a lady,
Well-bred, but right
On all occasions; at ninety
Lay in her bed putting
Death down:

I won't die.
We have had this argument
Before and you are quite
Mistaken. I won't die.
Eventually, he being no
Apostate, but an expert
Keeper of the faith,
She died where she lay,
Leaving the argument—
As she would say—
Unfinished. (She was
Right on all occasions.)

She may have lost the argument, but the exertion of will, employing active volition, was a manifestation, a resumption, of life. I had to begin to be rebellious and, hence, affirmative.

What had happened to me had been more than a simple shift, alteration, or modification. I had been made different, re-created through chance. An individual is not an assemblage of parts; when something is altered, everything changes. My body, then, was a partially sensate piece of modern art, an *objet trouvé* from the city dump. But change—to be useful, enduring, and real—must support the relationship between the past self-image and the new, modified one. To abandon one's previous totality as over or finished is an act of suicide; to be forced to abandon it is murder—unless the instigation is not done by a person but, rather, is the application of an objective force such as the strike of lightening, the broken dam, or the horse's hoof caught in the field mouse's hole. Murder requires the attribution of responsibility; death or abolition from external, amorphous powers does not. Defined that way, the incident becomes "fate" and is assumed to be uncontrollable, although, for Americans at least, that assumption requires an almost unachievable psychological state. Like the cancer victim described earlier, as a means of making sense out of the senseless, we tend to blame ourselves rather than accidents or abstractions such as God.

To continue to be oneself, the individual's priorities of self-constants must be maintained. Otherwise, the identity of the person is lost in transition. Without memory, with limited sight and hearing, surrounded by social and intellectual fog and obscurity, I was exploring myself, recognizing, defining, and mapping as I went. Even complete and in health, self-understanding is complex. It is as if parts of ourselves were separate witnesses to the others. Alan Watts put this condition in rhyme:

> There was a young man who said, "Though
> It seems that I know that I know,
> What I *would* like to see
> Is the "I" that knows "me"
> When I *know* that I know that I know.*

I was just reaching the first stage of this succession, beginning to know what I did not know.

Confronted with a wall-to-wall bathroom mirror, at first I

*Alan Watts, *The Book: On the Taboo against Knowing Who You Are*, p. 50.

did not recognize myself and turned away. My self-image had not been adapted to the massive changes, and for many months I avoided this reality: combing my hair in the mirrorless bedroom, going completely without make-up except for a colorless lipstick I could put on without light or glass. I could not really deceive myself; the illusion of my former physical being was not persistent enough. The painfulness did not derive from confusion about my identity but, rather, from knowing too well what I had become.

Coming home from the hospital I had been filled with an anserine—silly—euphoria. I had no struggle because I had no awareness of reality then. And when I did know, I was unable to accept my situation and so to gain the false peace of despair. Refusal kept me struggling and, thus, in active pain. Freya Stark, in old age, wrote that "that which breathes in the human heroism, separating it from everyday courage, is the *expectation and acceptance* of defeat." Some have the courage to build what they know will fall. That is an appealing thought, but it is not a possibility for me. Knowing I am doomed, I may have to *expect* it, but I will never *accept* it.

I doubt that anyone believes his or her body is perfect, inside or out, in workings or in appearance. But we grow accustomed to what we are, take it for granted, and trust it. When it proves untrustworthy, the loss is profound—almost as if perfection had become imperfect, solid virtue marred by decaying seams. I became ineffective, dependent, and, in my own eyes, asexual, and *in*-valid. What happened to me emotionally may have had more effect on my self—my person—than the malign disease. It followed a pattern of dynamic states that was new to me but one experienced over and over again by those disabled by accident or illness. First, with increasing awareness I became shocked by what I learned, filled with a sense of loss and sorrow. I could not deny what changes I recognized; I was saddened in a still, tight way. It was indicative of the depth of my distress that I could not cry, for tears are a healing release, serving to fructify the self as rains do for the earth, restoring and feeding the life principle.

As time went by and I became more conscious, I also became *angry*. In a response often reported by others in the past, I found myself experiencing the existential outrage that follows from having no one to blame for encompassing misfortune. I had to deal with the forces of evil—both powerful metaphysical ones and plain, everyday social values that made me despise my lacking, limited self.

Every time I reeled down the sidewalk, hit my head or another part of my body on my blind side, or could not remember my own address or telephone number, I knew that this was not how I *should* be, that I was defective. To bear the assumptions that others made from these incidents and not to be caught in them yourself—that is the response that must be learned. And it is not learned easily, though the pain from a fall or a knock may be ignored in the fire of the rage it inspires.

Does anger keep one alive? Maybe the feeling of any strong emotion can help to do that. And maybe it can be a useful exercise to pretend to feel it because by fakery and exercise it can become real.

There are, after all, a limited number of possible reactions to misfortune: *suicide, acceptance, planned public pretense, and anger*. The most dramatic is *quitting*—blowing your brains out or, more quietly, taking poison. The others are less extreme, if not a lot more satisfactory. Surely, there has to be more than resignation or acceptance! I have to be pleased (oh, the latent narcissist!) or, at least, satisfied with what I am and not just willing to be consoled by what is left. I am not very good at determined cheer, putting on a social front pretending that all is well. Rage has its uses. Many writers believe that anger is one of the most powerful forces that the newly disabled have at their command, that it is an energy stimulator and an antidote to the depression that can turn into passive suicide.

As I became somewhat aware of my disabilities, my limitations seemed real but not necessarily permanent. Progress, however slight, generated optimism. But, as I got better and then realized how crippled I was, I nearly drowned in a sense of futility and despair. Self-pity can be a fatal disease in itself. When I recognized the facts, I detested what I had to acknowledge. There is no way of thinking positively about tragedy— at least not on the spot. In due time what cannot be changed can be accepted and managed, if not mastered, so that it is no more than an intruding inconvenience. Part of coping with this management is the process of sorting out problems; dealing with small ones builds confidence for the larger tasks. Practice in using the coping mechanisms is absolutely necessary—so much so that overprotection can be devastating. We have all got to find an armamentarium of survival skills and *use* it—or rot, not caring if we are still alive or not.

I did not want to be blamed, and I did not want to be pitied. I was filled with great uneasiness at the thought of appearing pathetic or needful to others. Learning to take help was not easy; it was an admission of need. The ability to accept it—or, even more difficult, to elicit it when needed—was a long step forward from devaluing myself. Sometimes that taking may seem selfish, but not being able to do so can be a real hindrance in moving out of a dark corner into social daylight. One small example may make this clearer: Every time I left home I got lost. I hated asking directions when I knew that I was only a few blocks away from home. I was humiliated by my failure of memory, but I had to accept it, be lost in indefinite, wandering limbo, or stay stranded, in isolated safety at home. Laughing self-consciously, I asked.

From the beginning, progress had been erratic and unpredictable. I tried not to review it daily but, rather, about once a month. I needed to believe in positive change in order to keep working at it. (Even when I reached what felt to me like a permanent plateau—last winter—my doctor insisted that I was still recovering but at a slower pace.) If I were going to play the "mañana" game—Scarlett O'Hara's "I'll think about that tomorrow"—I had to believe that there would be time and opportunity to do that. Unless one is able to live fully in the present, the future is a hoax. But if today is *all* there is, this kind of thinking is only a general street cleaning, clearing away the debris for the moment. Planning and sequence were not possible; the present was stripped of the future, empty indeed. I was suffering from resentment—from the Latin, *resentire*, "to feel all over again." The dying take refuge within themselves, in dreams and hallucinations. With no such access, I stumbled on into life.

6

STRUGGLE

The image of rebirth, of deep and profound transformation,
is the counterpart of the imagery of death.

—ROBERT JAY LIFTON AND ERIC OLSON

For the first year of my recovery, I visited my doctor every
month, weighing in and having laboratory tests to check the
progress of my mending and the effects of the medicine I
continued to take—some of it for a full three years. (For a long
time I was investing about seventy-five dollars a month on a
variety of daily pills—an order that I filled once for about three
dollars in Canada, which is under a much more enlightened
national medical system.) My TB specialist was Robert Winters. When I heard later that his students at UCLA called this
attractive, competent professional "Dr. Bob," I decided that
he had earned the nickname by treating them and his other
patients the way he did me: with a paternal concern which
included guidance on life style and attitude as well as direct
medical care.

On every return to his office, I touched each of my fingers
with the thumb on the same hand; I followed white stripes on
a black band moved from left to right and back again in front
of my eyes. I performed other rituals on demand, some of

which were meaningful only to the observant doctor, but one of which was a symbolic exemplar of my condition from the first office visit and, like the weight scale, marked progress so clearly that I looked forward to it, sure each month (after the first three or four) of perceptible progress being made and recorded. This was a simple test: I was asked only to walk across the examination room without holding on, placing one foot in front of the other. Does it sound easy? Indeed, it is—*if* you are healthy, complete, and normally coordinated.

In the beginning I could barely stand up, even holding on. With increasing pride I began to show improvement—first, several wobbling steps more side by side than one ahead of the other; then, a gradual change in speed and balance until I reached the capability that I have now and am unlikely to better in the future, regardless of practice. Today, in full daylight and on level ground, I am in no fear of falling. One foot can be placed ahead of the other but somewhat offside, and I can go quickly and tippily about as far as I like—some miles when the land surface is not too rough and the vegetation not too abundant. As a measurable victory, the change has been reinforcing: it is *obvious.*

When I came home from the hospital, an enormous stack of mail—personal and professional—awaited my attention. I began to go through it slowly, not really involved. For a while I was utterly stable, not even bored with my static, humdrum being. Each day was a repetition. I was afloat in an unchanging miasma of gentle swells, ebbs, and flows. Nothing was possible; nothing incipient. Past plans were out of date, forgotten river routes and the present course and shore terrain too unfamiliar for prospective planning. Anticipation was impossible.

All of my senses were muted. I was in abeyance, suspended always in an enclosed state of separation like the first few moments of disorientated consciousness when a traveler awakens in a strange bed, a foreign room. Even my close environment was at a distance, strained through layers of effort to be recorded sensually. I could smell and feel, taste with daily increasing pleasure and awareness, but my sight and my hearing were much altered. The stars were gone as if they had never existed; distant three dimensions melted into an unreal blur.

From both eyes (although greatly increased in size in the right one) a mammoth triangular range of vision had been obliterated. Mapped with a white-tipped pointer on a hanging black chart in the ophthalmologist's office, it looked like this:

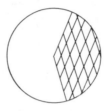

My visual field had been limited in such a way that I had to turn my head or I could not see anything or any person by my side. I walked into open doors, windows swung outward, tree trunks, cars, passers-by, bruising myself black and blue, not knowing they were there. On the right side of my glasses, a vertically striped, transparent band was affixed to extend my vision. I had to learn to use it properly—there was a field of overlap and a general sense of looking around corners! In due time, this clever device made it possible for me to learn to drive again.

Lack of directionality in lowered hearing did not help the vision loss either; I could not hear what I was not seeing. I had been completely deaf in one ear from early childhood; three mastoid operations were attempts to cope with repeated infections, but they had not changed my restricted hearing. With the tubercular meningitis I had lost hearing in my remaining "good" ear, the one I had depended on solely for years. Once before I had tried a hearing aid but without success, and, while I had thought it would be a welcomed enhancement, I had not believed it all that necessary. But now things were different. The hearing loss was no longer just the annoyance of missing clues in a crowded room of speakers or from a soft-spoken friend standing or sitting on my deaf right side. The audiologist began by suggesting that I try a bilateral model. In the partially functioning ear, I was to wear an aid that attached around the back of my head to the deaf ear. From the beginning, I knew that, barring even greater hearing loss, I would not wear that blatant advertisement of disability!

Fortunately, he tested my long-nonresponsive organ and quickly decided that a tiny, recently developed model using a silver oxide battery seated directly behind the ear would be most effective. It was out of sight but very present in mind! Since I could not remember ever hearing with that ear, the result was unimaginable: I could hear voices and vehicles, movement behind me and to the right, even half a block away, wind in the bushes and branches, the barking of warning dogs, purring of self-satisfied pussycats, and, as I walked, the endless twitterings of birds and song in once-silent spaces. I heard voices and movement far to my right; the noise of accelerating trucks and other moving traffic suddenly became an intrusion. The dimensions of my physical environment had deepened and become a complicated means of sensual contact. Stereo music had an entirely new meaning. Because of my illness, I have acquired an access to sound I might never have found without the special incentive to look for it. A dormant section of my body has awakened.

In that great mass of mail accumulated while I was in the hospital was an invitation to attend a small theory conference being sponsored by the Association for Humanistic Psychology in Tucson early that year. I had belonged to this organization for some years, had attended conferences in Europe, Hawaii, and many parts of the United States, and had always enjoyed myself without being able to shed the feeling that it was a complicated conglomerate or social mass of persons each suffering from the delusion that the field of humanistic psychology was readily definable and that its definition and underlying values were widely shared. For most professional humanistic psychologists, philosophy and not empiricism had been their central concern. This conference, supported by the National Endowment for the Humanities, was being held as an attempt to vitalize theory and research in the field.

I was delighted to have been included and, although the acceptance date was past, made up my mind to go if the possibility still existed. The decision was a mark of my personal distance from reality. I anticipated most interesting interaction with these gifted colleagues (many of whom I had never met, although I had been familiar with their work). I did *not* anticipate the results of the present limitations: what I heard I did not understand or remember, even as little as several minutes later. The individuals I had known—even for years—had to introduce themselves to me. (One of those unrecognized—I realized only months later when I came across our past correspondence in my files—had been close friend and lover.)

I suspect now that I was probably perceived as an inhibited snob rather than disabled. No one there, except Rollo May, knew that I had been ill.

The two-day meeting was held in a garden hotel within the city; each time I stepped from my room I was lost—lost in the dining room, in the entrance, and, after dark or during the day, crossing the garden to get from meeting place to meeting place. The limits of the space in which I was operating cognitively were about four feet in each direction from my physical presence. No maps beyond that were possible. I did not want to be spoken to because I could not reply. Why? Aside from the vast lacunae of words, I simply did not remember what had just been said to me! An opinion was asked of each of us around the circle in which we sat: I panicked with the questioner's approach, stuttered in my inadequacy and resolutely avoided noting the reactions to what I had said. Thin, silent, and cane-carrying, I was my own news release. I gained little and contributed nothing, went away longing for contact and knowing it impossible.

In some ways, this episode was typical of my bumpy progress on the road to recovery. Over and over again I was invited to attend, to speak, to participate or perform because of a reputation for competencies that no longer existed. I went out in public thoroughly unable to communicate—receive *or* send—effectively, and over the next three years (although with some increasing powers) I did this again and again—in appearances and performances (to me, at least) so obviously defective that I was sure my necessary professional image was being destroyed. I knew that I should have refrained from such nonsensical behavior, but I could not—and I did not. Those who did not know me from before could hardly have valued me; those who did were quietly nonjudgmental and supportive. No one said, "Go home and wait, go home and practice, rebuilding old skills and learning new ones," and perhaps they did not because they could not know, any more than I did, *whether waiting, rereading, and practicing would do any good.*

Almost a year later a memorial conference for Sidney Jourard was held at the University of Florida in Gainesville, and I was invited to participate. Sid, a gifted investigator of aspects of the self, had recently been killed in a bizarre accident while he was working on his car. In a series of meetings, speakers were asked to deliver talks which would then, usually in developed form, be collected within a single volume and published. Doing nothing else professionally, I worked on my paper and chapter for *two* months, my labors constantly interrupted by an expired attention span of roughly *fifteen minutes*. Even then the task would have been impossible had I not thoroughly plagiarized from my own previously published work. I was no longer *completely* out of contact; the contact was still intermittent, but it had become a real *possibility*. I began to have my first shoots of belief in a scholarly future resumed.

These two conferences were developmental landmarks for me. At home past social connections were lost and interaction greatly diminished. I was finding insulation in my alienation and using that place as a haven of self-defense. Each step along the way to even a moronic competency was a labored, deliberate attempt to reclaim past knowledge. As if I had not lived in that location for five years, I had to relearn the names of streets and where they joined or crossed, the location of public buildings, parks, and stores—and, once inside, how to sort out their contents and shelves, not get stranded in the aisles or corridors, and be able to find the doors, to leave as well as to enter. I learned to use a checklist as a mnemonic inventory of identifiable things, tagged items into limited collections that were meaningful only to me.

I learned that knowing was not for knowing's sake but for the sake of control, for access to power, to the ability to *do*.

And what petty actions I had to accomplish to create breathing space! I even had to learn how to make a phone call. (Write the name of the person being called on a slip of paper and, beside it, the number. Hold the paper in front of you for continued reference. If you put it down, you will have to hang up the telephone and start over again.) Without the prompt, seven consecutive numbers could not be remembered long enough to dial a call.

The location of kitchen equipment, utensils, and foods was another problem. My cupboards and closet shelves were alien lands being visited for the first time over and over again. I had no trouble with consecutive letters, though, and I arranged the herbs, spices, and condiments in alphabetical order so I could find them. I did not try this in the beginning, however, and I doubt that it would have worked then. Just out of the hospital, my series difficulties were consistent: dialing, I could not remember the number I had just touched; spelling, I did not know how far I had gotten and so what letter was next; and, listening, I could not recall to what I was responding—or even what I had already said.

The walls were constantly falling into an internal confusion without din, a blank darkness obscuring hearing and vision. Somehow physical inabilities were more readily coped with than mental ones. Even in derelict ruins my body was not to be abandoned as an uninhabitable city. I have learned so much about the capacity of the human body to defray the expenses of invasion or accident. Coping does not end until the final stillness; the force of will continues, even in unconsciousness, and I believe that it must often be the operant factor in any outcome of life or death. Earlier I had seen this in my sister Gay's intense holding battles with her defective heart. I had recorded it in poetry and in my journal.

In 1956, my father had a devastating accident while on expedition in the Brazilian jungles along the Amazon River. In preparation for the night camp, trees were being felled and a clearing made in the complex shore tangles. When the foreman gave the order for the action to stop, one worker, not hearing, failed to do so. When the tree came down, it carried my father to the ground as well, with multiple injuries to him, including a fractured skull and leg. In the past, in that environment of heat and humidity, which spurs the growth of gangrene and body poisons, such an injury was a death sentence. Treated immediately with penicillin, he was placed in an open boat, paddled furiously toward Manaos, and, about twenty-four hours out, transferred to a passing power launch.

Endless difficulties followed (some of which have been described in his unconventional autobiography).* Once they had arrived in the city, Pan American Airline refused to take on a passenger whom their personnel perceived to be dying and finally conceded when a local doctor was obtained to accompany him on the flight back to New York City. Airline information on the landing of the flight was confused, and my mother (with the ambulance to carry my father to the hospital) went first to one airport and then to the other. What must have seemed like endless operations, pain, and incapacity (culminating in an unbendable, permanently aching leg) followed for several years, tempered only by the steady strength of the inner will to live and to mend. Medical resources alone would not have kept him alive; his physical being responded to the insistent spirit within.

So it was—in modified, simpler form—in my own case as well. My investment in healing was high—hard, ceaseless work —and I was aided, mysteriously, from within as well as by my medications. Every step of the recovery, self-consciously marked and pondered, was indicative of this collaboration. One small example was the manifestation of my menstrual cycle. Since I had my first period—beginning on Easter Sunday, when I was thirteen years old, and duly recorded—except for

*George Gaylord Simpson, *Concession to the Improbable* (New Haven: Yale University Press, 1978).

the months of three pregnancies, I had menstruated regularly, with no unusual ebb or flow or pain. This had been true, I believe, of all those years before my illness. After I returned home from the hospital and heard how I had been cared for in so many ways—including hair washing and physical therapy while I was unconscious—I had wondered how my family or the nursing staff had managed this additional complication. It soon became obvious to me: this body, in battle for its life, was not concerned with the mechanisms of reproduction. The factory had closed.

When I began to realize this, I simply assumed that it had happened this way for a combination of reasons. The first, of course, was my illness; the second, my age. I had had no symptoms of menopause yet, but somehow it seemed perfectly possible and, in fact, extraordinarily tidy, for what was usually a slowing and irregular process of some years to be collapsed and condensed under these circumstances. I accepted the change, then, with equanimity since I had been expecting it in another, more conventional form.

The human body is the outward expression of individual conditions. It has an extraordinary capacity to focus on the physical functions needed for immediate survival. I know now that this is a common historical happening. Under extreme conditions the reproductive mechanisms are extraneous and irrelevant; they have nothing to do with maintenance *now*, at that present time. The door to the future is closed when women stop menstruating, but, when that happens, other necessary life forces can be marshaled and utilized for continuation in the present. The female survivors of the Nazi concentration camps were combating external disaster, a comprehensively pernicious environment whose effects extended far beyond the physical; I was trying to repel an internal attack which was usurping the authority of my body. In both cases, the response was an unconscious rally, a self-protective measure utilizing all the available weaponry of the whole person. In both cases we stopped menstruating.

As it turned out later, however, my interpretation that menstruation had ended permanently was quite wrong. My body processes were merely undergoing a prolonged therapeutic hiatus, which ended about a year and a half after my illness, when, to my amazement, the flows began again—not as regularly at first, but with the clear, healthful purpose they had always had. To me, this resumption was a landmark of resurgent vitality, and, in spite of the concomitant nuisance, I welcomed it.

With a sustained faith in my recuperative powers, from the beginning I was willing to work at change. From the wheelchair, I stepped out with the metal-frame walker. Surrounding me on three sides, it seemed much more supportive and solid than crutches could have been. When I was promoted to a cane, I was sure that I would fall, and, with practice, I learned how to do it easily, usually without injury, and then to try to avoid it. (I still fall today, but much less frequently, less painfully.) I moved slowly, swerving all over the sidewalk, counting the steps, then the city blocks and the amount of time it took to traverse them. Each added increment, however small, was a triumph. Then I bought a pedometer and began to keep records. Friends and my children walked with me, grasping one arm for balance, so that the dependence on the slight stick by my side was minimized. Eventually we walked in the state parks over hills this way, looked down into the mountain valleys, the bursting city of Los Angeles, the seemingly unoccupied sea, and called it "hiking."

Every day I went to the palisade park. What in the beginning felt like a private and personal domain was actually the well-populated activity grounds of consistent retirees or the wounded: walking or wheeled-disabled. They appeared every day—as if the greens were extensions of their own back yards —with folded tables and chairs, sun umbrellas, hampers of food and drink and open purses carrying newspapers, pencils for crossword puzzles and writing paper, radios, knitting, or other handwork, and cards for the endless games.

I walked, leaning, with the walker or cane, then seated myself on a bench. (Choosing the grass to sit on might have meant a permanent commitment to the spot; I was still too weak to get up without assistance.) Neither dogs nor bicyclists were allowed, but occasionally one or the other came by among the strolling visitors. One pair of men came out during their lunch hour, striding from the wharf to the end of the park to the north and back again every day. They always smiled and waved; often they stopped to talk.

The beauty of the waters—Catalina Island faintly offshore —the arcs of the beaches and the wild thrust of the Santa Monica Mountains close by, curving into the sea, were far from soothing. I was raw, susceptibilities exposed, my tenderness and sensitivity to feelings constantly, helplessly aroused. What I had seen before, responded to but held at a distance, had suddenly taken on penetrating powers. The result was painful.

Many of the retirees or disabled whom I met in the park were friendly, wanting to talk, to exchange grievances and their restricted lives. Most assumed that I had been in an accident; all knew that, whatever their origin, our disabilities made us a community. It was less our real limitations than the shared stigma that created a universe of response among us. We were different and, therefore, in many ways segregated, suffering the penalty of isolation. Stereotyped by others, not as an act of malice but, rather, through an ordinary process of short-cut generalization, the false summary labels were applied to ourselves by us, too: social stigma is a basis for self-concept and the loss of self-esteem.

We are all shackled by social categories; generalizing labels are inescapable and always untrue. But I was far more disabled than these invalids and cripples, far more incapacitated, crippled, handicapped, and invalid. I was afraid of being rejected, but *even more so* of being accepted, by them. I needed to believe that they were "different." And I was afraid that they could smell my cowardly withdrawal when I called out at a distance and continued on my way.

In the beginning, still in the metal walker, I welcomed their contact; in time I came to think of them as heroes of adjustment. They had learned two basic truths that are common knowledge among the spokespersons for the disabled: that to be physically handicapped and alone is to be doubly disadvantaged and that the disabled can be independent without being isolated. No one can afford to abandon the social world defensively, to hide behind sheltering, distancing walls, to think of himself or herself as belonging to an underprivileged class separated in disease-maintaining environments. Many of them see themselves as members of a group that is capable of changing its status through connection and solidarity among its members.

Not just those I met personally there, but all the disabled needed me as one of the many human tools operating toward the accomplishment of group political ends; I needed them as individual role models whose matter-of-fact endurance shamed away destructive self-pity. Self-defense begins with the truth. I needed to be able to admit that this was the way I *really* was then—even if I hoped it would not always be so.

But very quickly I became afraid and not rejecting, but avoiding. I never met anyone who had survived the disease I had. But, regardless of what their problems were, I did not want to be admitted to their motley company, to be identified as "one of them." The search for like company is an admission that you belong with the others you seek, that you are similar. I was trying desperately to define my self differently. I became a disaffiliate, declining voluntarily to accept the social place accorded me.

If I had known the extent of my own disability, accepted its reality and the fact that it could be lasting (indeed, life-long), I could have accepted their warm outreach as supportive and joined the boundless club, offering my own conscious limitations as the basis for membership. But I did not want to have to cope; I wanted to forget, to develop the capacity to disregard, to be indifferent to these new qualities of my self. These honest feelings were complicated by self-contempt; how ignoble of me to reject the inclusion, the support they offered!

I was far more uneasy with others than I was alone, never feeling that I was able to do an adequate job of protecting my self-image. I had no vanity about my past physical resources or beauty because I did not remember them, but it was inconceivable that my self should be impaired. I began to hate people with infirmities with an unending dogmatic strength, refusing to be identified with them. By doing this, I was avoiding thinking of myself as unwholesome and bungled. The deforming experience *need* not lead to the development of a deformed personality any more than all disease has to terminate in permanent physical or emotional disorder. But there is a real talent in the ability to live with physical infirmity without being corroded by it. John Merrick, encased in the degradation of his Elephant Man body, was able to say, with almost a sense of ecstasy, "I am happy every hour of the day." Such nobility of the spirit! It is almost unimaginable.

In part the ability to trust myself to mend and to adapt to

what could not be mended has grown from others who have experienced similar crises and described them in writing. For me, print and paper made my access to them much less anxiety-producing than the demands of the friendly disabled whom I met on my walks. I certainly recognized what I was told on the pages—that, for everyone caught in this trap of limitation, the sense of personal disaster leads to the continued expectation of helplessness and so to passivity, sadness, cognitive deficits, and low self-esteem. *(Low self-esteem!* How much more formal that sounds than *self-rejection* or *self-hating!)*

What happens is the development of a specific attributional style: belief by the person afflicted that the cause of this misfortune was *internal* ("I did it to myself"), that it is a *stable* condition ("It's going to last forever"), and that its effects would be *all-encompassing* or *global* ("It will undermine everything important to me"). Over time, as I read and began to talk to the injured, the maimed, the limited, I began to realize the underlying commonalities of what superficially appeared to be highly idiosyncratic experiences. Not then, but much later, I came to realize the universality of the community to which I had gained such unwilling access. As Erving Goffman wrote,

> . . . it is not very useful to tabulate the numbers of persons who suffer the human predicament . . . the number would be as high as one wanted to make it . . . the issue becomes not whether a person has experience with a stigma of his own, because he has, but rather how many varieties he has had his own experience with.*

Eventually my fear of being like the obviously disabled diminished, partly because the methods of coping with each of

*Erving Goffman, *Stigma: Notes on the Management of Spoiled Identity* (Englewood Cliffs, N.J.: Prentice-Hall, 1963), p. 129.

these stages of helplessness were different. What the individual, the person, *was* interacted strongly to modify the effects of what happened to him or her.

Eleanor Clark questioned eloquently the reasons for her failing eyesight:

> Did I ever abuse the heart's ̮wild intake of certain joy and wonder, a counterradiance, in all that white-gold splendor as we glide heavenward, God's grandeur in shook foil around us past the screen of obscenities—woods and packed slope of such different handling in the brilliance, as unlike as hawk-skilled skiers swooping are from the brute crashers-down or the simply cautious or inexperienced who make their turns like ferryboats—did I let love, of motion and bright air, be more than was fitting, for it to lead to this far swifter shadowing in?*

Like her and many others who have suffered from serious illness, I did wonder if I were to blame, if I had caused my illness—through overwork and anxiety about it. I coped by radical avoidance with the fear that my disability was a stable condition bound to last forever. At first I was literally thoughtless and happy—or at least neutral in my nonthinking. Then, as thought crept into consciousness, I denied my difficulties. Later, measuring and recording infinitesimal changes made it possible for me to believe in the potential return to normalcy and to convince myself that the destructive effects I was experiencing would be comprehensive only temporarily.

Psychologist C. Scott Moss remarked about his own recovery from stroke-caused aphasia, that being a perfectionist with high self-imposed standards made him hypersensitive about his disabilities, real or imagined, and, therefore, strive mightily to

---

*Eleanor Clark, *Eyes, etc.: A Memoir* (New York: Pocket Books, 1977), p. 48.

get over them.* People who have had strokes have lost the outward manifestation of speech but not the internal aspects of thought. My situation was much more inclusive since I could not complete sentences or make sense in the way that I combined words, *and* I could not think—organize the resources that would allow me to communicate verbally with others. I had not lost the information I had, but I had lost access to it. Moss's intelligence was unimpaired, but he had no means of expressing it. He could not speak. In his book he tells an anecdote about a malicious God who made the porpoise intelligent but gave it no means of expression for the gift. What agony for the beast, but how much more so for the man to know that he had an ability and was not able to use it to communicate!

It seems to me that the greatest liability for most of the disabled must be in the constriction of the future. My situation was different. I was a two-dimensional cripple since I had lost my past as well as my prospects. The newly handicapped mourn because they are unable to sever their ties with the past. I had nothing to mourn; what was behind me was completely gone. It could not be recalled to be remembered, cherished, or missed. I had escaped what Arthur Fielding called "the sad and awful fact of knowing, and of remembering, of knowing and retaining too well the lethal, internal artifact of certain pasts." For me, the beginning of the future had to become rooted in the experienced, present day; it could not be a leftover of planning from earlier days. From a well-mapped future nothing remained at all for these three years. Then, gradually, I began to learn how to relieve this constriction—to explore, to hope, to believe that I would return wholly.

*C. Scott Moss, *Recovery with Aphasia: The Aftermath of My Stroke* (Urbana: University of Illinois Press, 1972), p. 192.

Realism is the invented product of personality. Reality was what *I* made it—within limits. Some things I had to accept even if they had been unimaginable in the past: the reality of death and disabling illness and the inability of the individual to choose to control them. You can decide *how* you will do what you *can* do but you *cannot choose what those things will be.* Some of us can pretend that we owe nothing to anyone, but survivors know we need each other.

7

CONSTITUTIONAL AMENDMENT

Bear in mind that "to heal" does not
necessarily imply "to cure." It can mean
simply helping a patient to achieve a way
of life compatible with his own aspira-
tions, even though his disease continues.

—RENÉ DUBOS

It did not occur to me until long after my hospitalization that
I might have been responsible for my illness. I do think now
that I had probably not taken proper care of myself—appropriate food, relaxation, exercise, company—as I should have. But
how I felt then about my life, my work, the daily trials and
ventures in my relationships with others, I do not know now.
Was I doing what I wanted to do? How I wanted to do it?
With whom? Was I happy? Contented? Pleased with myself?
I do not know.

As I began to read the works of others who had been gravely
ill, I realized that there was a pattern among them: these
writers consistently tended to believe that their illnesses were
brought on by something they were doing (or not doing) and

that they were to blame. The inexplicable had to be explained. They were attacked by strong feelings of guilt, feelings not supported by evidence or logic. In order to find some meaning in what had happened to them, they were doing what psychologists have labeled "blaming the victim." If there is not any readily accessible explanation for misfortune, then the easiest way to cope with it may be to say, "It served him or her—or me—right!"

Sometimes this emphasis is referred to as a form of medical evangelism in which old-fashioned sin is replaced by depression, repression, and denial. Redemption requires confession and an altered life style. A religious metaphor is sometimes used: "rebirth" into health. If you blame someone else or external forces, then you are accepting your own helplessness; if you are responsible, then it must be because you have the power to change the situation. Recent preventive or "prospective" medicine places a great deal of responsibility on the individual for his or her own health—*responsibility*, but not *blame*.

The practice of holistic medicine, as it is advocated today, would make both health and illness very different experiences from what they have been in the past. Humans are being redefined as having the capacity to heal themselves—to mend or amend their own constitutions. They are respected as active partners in health care, not as the passive recipients of it. According to James Gordon, who has laid out a complete paradigm of holistic medicine,* the field addresses itself to the mental, emotional, social, and spiritual aspects, as well as the biological ones, of the physical beings who come for care. For

*James Gordon, "The Paradigm of Holistic Medicine," in *Health for the Whole Person*, ed. A. C. Hastings, J. Fadiman, and J. S. Gordon (Boulder, Col.: Westview Press, 1980), pp. 3–27.

the client, this view produces quite a different experience from that of having a specific area of the body under study *by itself.* Statistical studies are appreciated for their predictive value in generalizing about groups, but treatment has to be tailored to each patient's unique needs and individual genetic, biological, and psychosocial background. This means, of course, that people have to be treated in the context of their own cultures, families, and communities, and not those of the doctor.

Most important, emphasis is on the promotion of health as a definable, positive state *in itself* and not as the *absence* of disease. Insofar as possible, illness is to be prevented, not treated, and it is the responsibility of the individual to maintain his or her own health.

Self-responsibility means taking charge of one's own management, acting on one's own behalf, using professional resources as means to individual self-care. In a world of massively unequal distribution of resources, individual responsibility alone would be meaningless without commitment to change those social and economic conditions that perpetuate ill health. I was told that I had a "slum" disease. If *I* could get it—living the way I did—how many more suffer unnecessarily in crowded, unhealthy conditions?

Three stages in metaphor make clear the way that medicine, as a field of human endeavor, has evolved from after-the-fact coping with illness and injury to their prevention. Many years ago the victim of a fall from a rocky ledge would have been comforted as he died and his remains appropriately disposed of. In more recent times he might have been caught mid-flight by carefully positioned nets. Today his physician might be at the top of the cliff with him, checking his state of mind, food intake, physical fitness, spiritual and social standing, as well as his capacity for balance. As a consequence, he may not fall at all; but, if he does, it will not be a matter of professional indifference, ignorance, or personal neglect. And, as a result of contemporary changes in his upbringing, he will have internal resources to control his landing in the net and to manage his life afterward.

I do believe that I had the best medical care available anywhere in the world: intelligent, careful, well-educated, experienced doctors and the most recent equipment and other resources for their use. But when I went home from the hospital, I was still caught in that saving net. Beyond a certain point the medical practitioners did not help my transition back to full functioning—because their professional interests and training were simply too narrow.

My physicians were not so distant from me that I felt their lofty estate was intended to keep me in my place. I never felt devalued, condescended to, or paternalized. But learned professional detachment kept these doctors from being emotional resources for me, a stance that can be altered by a change in values in medical school, where the physician-patient relationship is defined and taught. I never felt, however, that they were indifferent or contemptuous, that they were falsifying information—although, as time went on, I *did* wonder if they were *withholding* it.

Today I believe that my physicians did not lay out an expected route of progress for me for a number of reasons. Competent and self-assured, my TB specialist was nevertheless without the towering sense of authority that might have prevented him from seeking others' advice or repeatedly trying tentative remedies and altering them when they failed to work. Unlike the insensitive doctor about whom a friend recently told me, he was not about to list what I would never do again and, in that way, to set up a self-fulfilling prophecy. "If I need lies to cheer me, I'll take gloom," Eleanor Clark wrote when she thought she was going blind. But believable, *believed* lies can be useful if they prevent despair and the abandonment of effort.

They did not lie to me, but neither did the doctors tell me what capacities would certainly come back. At first I believed their silence was tactful, the desire to let me find out slowly and hence more bearably. Later I came to realize that their silence and hesitation—the fact that they were qualifying everything that was said—were simply reflections of their own uncertain knowledge. Every patient is unique, every manifestation of illness distinct in some way. This was certainly true of the invasion in my brain. There are parts of everyone's brain that are silent, that can be damaged or removed with no detectable neurological deficit. But most of it is vital, even within millimeters.

A skull is more imaginably human than a brain. Could Hamlet have picked up the dead man's *brain* and addressed it: "Alas, poor Yorick!"? A brain is like the wind; its *effects* are what you see. The immense journey toward complete knowledge of the brain has just begun. The doctors did not know; they did not understand all that had happened to me. An open acknowledgment of that ignorance at the time would have been helpful to no one. While others tried to hold me, my life hung precariously from their hands.

This traditional net-providing medical model of human functioning may have been necessary in the past; today it seems reductionist. It minimizes the capacities of the ordinary person; it covertly encourages dependency on external, specialized knowledge. I stumbled accidentally over a thriving alternative to this view which I later learned is called a "holistic health model." This is a model of the modern physician as a skilled practitioner who must attend to caring as well as curing—to treating the whole person and focusing upon preventive medicine, anticipating threats of disease, and maintaining health, rather than being compelled to restore it. What is proposed is assistance to help the person to live well until he or she dies. This is the model of the third stage in the metaphor given earlier—the physician helping the person at the top of the cliff.

In the past few years the use of this model has been greatly expanded. Beside the treatment for physical maladies, it involves the explicit search for self-discovery, a process that includes the setting of goals and the consideration and choice of means for achieving them. The tissues and the organ systems of the body are related to other systems within the human body, the family, and the culture. What is sought is harmonious interaction among all these systems, whether they are biological, social/political, or economic. The systems paradigm underlies much current thought about holistic health, all the aspects of human life impinging on each other and interacting, *causing* either disease or health. The word *health* itself is used as a metaphor for personal development and the increased control over life and its quality.

Health is abundance. Not simply the absence of illness or disease, it is the experience of plenty, of strength and vitality, actualizable possibility. But it is also the casting off of what is not vital and needed. When the Greeks spoke of *kenosis,* they were refering to an *emptying* process, to the need for less of confusion, obfuscation, multiplicity, and dissemblance. Small can be beautiful, all right (as Schumacher wrote), and the shedding process can be enabling. In health, the kenotic principle at work is orienting and centering. Reminiscent of the passive, receptive cognizing praised by Lao-tzu and the Eastern Taoistic philosophers, it is facilitating; described by Abraham Maslow, this state is a "desireless awareness"; by Kirshnamurti, a "choiceless" one. But in illness, when this casting off becomes involuntary and extreme, it is no longer valuable. It diminishes, reduces, and destroys.

Can anyone today believe that *curative* care is adequate? I, like all the disabled, should have been helped to master my environment, helped to understand that illness and health both derive from biological *and* social causes—pressures to do too much and to do it in life-limiting ways. More than sickness must be mended if health is to be achieved and to be lasting.

Any disorder is created out of a complex interaction of social factors, the presence of disease-producing elements in the environment, physical and psychological stress, the personality of the person subjected to these influences, and the inability of that person to adapt adequately to pressures. Some psychologists see illness as a maladaptive response to chronic, unresolved emotional stress. If that is the case, then "de-stressing" ought to make one well! Traditionally, doctors have taken it for granted that disease is not voluntary, a matter of choice or will power. But today some write about it as "context-dependent" behavior, behavior that happens in certain environments and not in others. Are there always two factors in the genesis of illness: pathological behavior of an organ or regulatory system and "illness" of the personal context—the family, the natural group? Does anyone become sick just because the sickness already exists in the larger world? Or are there also *host factors* (as the doctors call them) which contribute to the response to exposure? Was I biologically and psychologically ready to be host to invaders? Did I *invite* them?

Of course, I do not believe that this could be so literally. There is an element of chance or of luck in being either well or ill. But I do know that I was neglectful, and I do believe that responses to the social world have great influence on the body's performance. In a published interview Carl Simonton, the cancer specialist, attributed his own need to struggle with the disease to "loss of face." Where was the cancer located? On the skin of his face. A friend of mine whose close marriage of twenty-five years broke up in painful emotional disarray believes that his heart failure was the result of a "broken heart." But research on personality and cultural factors in disease is contradictory among groups of cancer victims. For example, one American study showed religiosity a common feature of women with breast cancer, but Japanese physicians found spontaneous regression among those of their patients who held deep religious faith.

The belief systems of the ill play a significant role in the personal management of disease. Charles Garfield deduced from his studies of cancer patients that those who survived were those who *chose* for optional peak performance, who believed that it was *possible*—that they could do it. It was not a choice made for them by outsiders. Every one of the cancer patients whom he studied was "absolutely sure he knew why he had survived," what it was that had kept him alive. *But none of them agreed with each other as to what those reasons were!* The one commonality was "an absolute, fierce belief in survival, a heightened placebo effect." They tended to participate in their process more than nonsurvivors did, attended to their nutrition, to developing internal ways of working against the illness, and saw themselves as fighters with positive attitudes and the will to live.

We have to believe in the mind's power to heal as well as the body's: prolonged anxiety and depression are both partial surrender to death. Emotional stress plays a part in any illness. How could it be any other way since mind and body are one? Anxiety and depression are experienced biologically in that unity.

Some people stay well because of a built-in hardiness, a kind of stress-resistant personality that is characterized by three C's:

challenge, commitment, and *control.* The person who has flexibility, an openness to change and challenge, gains beneficial effects from novelty and surprise. One who leads an engaged life has a feeling of involvement in whatever he or she is doing. And the individual who has a sense of control over events is less likely to be anxious or overreactive. (The same symptoms of stress occur during times of great joy as during negative, life-affecting events!)

Stress alone does not seem to make people ill. According to a study by a student of David McClelland, sickness seems to depend on whether the stress people are exposed to impinges on their basic motivations for power, achievement, and affiliation with others. What is encouraging about these findings is the suggestion that the attitudes and outlooks that affect health are largely *learned from experience* and, therefore, can be altered when the social situation is changed.

What distinguishes people who stay healthy? For many of them, first of all, healthy parents—a sound heredity. Second, their choice of occupation—some jobs have more time pressures, more physical danger, and greater need for consistent, tension-producing accuracy. Third, their social supports. The most potent protection from illness may be the closeness of a spouse. In England a recent study disclosed that widowers have a rate of illness 40 percent higher than their married counterparts. But married or not, individuals with relevant social ties to other human beings are healthier than others who lack such meaningful intercourse. Common-sense observations and statistics agree: a web of human relations—a network—nurtures and protects the individual.

Individual change does not automatically lead to needed social change. The step from personal commitment to new definitions of health and new health practices is only the first. The next is to link these single perceptions and changes into interpersonal networks in which the dialectical relationship between perceptions and stages of growth and development lead to synergistic, overall change—for *everyone* involved. That is, first we need a new understanding of what health really means; next, we need networks created to build human groups to serve as surrogate families to support and enhance the lives of all of their members.

Sometimes we shape the nature, course, and outcome of health and illness simply by the way we define them. Described to others or not, all our lives are fiction, creations encased in the trappings provided by the time and space within which they occur. The house of illness, where the story takes place, is the body. Since it was my own, it was no abstraction to me. But illness sucked definition from the body's workings even as it made them much more obvious, much less to be taken for granted. Their fragility was real but still subject to change as I rebuilt my strengths.

Weakness is not the same as being tired; the one prevents effort and the other is a result of it—even a very pleasant one. Physical fatigue—even for the slightest exertion—dwelt within that house and became a valued state of being, bringing a sweet emptiness which is very different from the neutrality of inertia or ineptitude. Step by step (sometimes quite literally—beginning to stand, trying to walk, then to run) what I was relearning to do used my muscles and all their back-up workings. It was physically tiring, and, therefore, as I accomplished it, relaxing and rest-producing.

But even accepting that you are responsible—at least partially—for the illness does not make it any easier to be responsible for getting well. It takes a long time to realize that working on recovery is a thing for the *mender* to do—not just for him or her *alone* (since specialized knowledge is also needed), but he or she must be actively involved and committed to the process. The silent boundaries the medical profession puts on its own responsibilities as a part of this process create a problem, especially when the long recovery really only begins when the patient leaves the hospital. The patient believes the doctor is going to do the rest of the job or instruct him or her in how to do it (or how to find out how to do it); the doctor believes that the client already knows what conditions he or she has to create and maintain in order to continue progress. Neither is true. "Nobody told me." Those words appear over and over again in the records of the ill who have recovered. And they apply here, too.

Perhaps at first, because I was so frail, no one told me what I could do to help rebuild myself: physical therapy, systematic exercise, tape recordings of my speech and reading patterns to have some clear way to describe and reference change, practice in speech and memory, writing and reading. All of these I came to by myself. The doctors were pleased when change became obvious and recordable. I was praised. Once they had granted me life, however, they had had nothing to do with guaranteeing its quality. It was as if they believed in the spontaneous recovery of my full powers once the malignant forces were dealt an initial heavy blow—and if lighter ones followed systematically.

Today, health professionals who approach their work holistically use a wide variety of personal resources to influence change in their clients. One of these is what my sister, Joan Burns, has called "positive framing"—seeking something within the environment that can frame one with good feelings. Norman Cousins, battling with a potentially lethal enemy, lay in bed and laughed himself well at daily showings of comic movies. Imagination is another one of these resources. In all illness there is a great interference with the imaginative processes, especially when there is high fever or physical suffering.

In delirium images are distorted. And in pain, how can I think of anything else if I am hurting so badly? There is a coarctation of the thought processes to the present, the here and now, step by step.

Can imaginative processes be evoked to lessen these restrictions? Carl Simonton, referred to earlier, uses the imagination of positive expectations in order to influence the immune-defensive system directly. Using guided imagery with his cancer patients, he asks each of them to visualize the opposing forces of disease and health at battle within the body. The visualization takes many forms, and the physical host—the body itself—that is the battleground is never neutral or unaffected. When the forces of health do not win in the visualization, the patient is desperately ill, and belief in recovery is faltering.

In his book on healing from within, psychologist Dennis Jaffe points out that the use of the patient's own "inner advisers" and relaxation training, as well as diagnostic and healing imagery, represents a departure from the orthodox conception of the doctor's role. It is, however, very much in keeping with the traditional practice of the folk healer of many other cultures. As medication, mental imagery has no negative side effects; rather, it mobilizes those inner powers of the person that have immense potential to aid in the healing and the promotion of health. This practice is a good example of how the observer's perspective modifies the object being observed.

Since I could not visualize at all, it was most fortunate for me that I suffered no pain.

My beliefs about the possibility of recovery, about the extent of recovery, and my belief that I could influence it grew stronger as time went by. But the beliefs of my physicians about me and about themselves have also been involved in my mending. The similarities between theirs and mine constitute important factors in the success of treatment. If I do not have faith in my doctor, agree with his diagnosis, his prescriptions and proscriptions, how can I be repaired by him? For me, both science and faith are necessary, but history is full of reports of healing based on faith alone—magical stories of cures at Lourdes, healings by suggestion, the use of placebos or nocebos in the treatment of psychogenically induced illness. There are tales of doctors who deceived others, but also of those who deceived themselves into aggrandizing their powers. Some were comfortable with the thought that just their being present to the ill was the medicine needed, not bottled drops or skillful incision.

We who are seriously ill draw on the faith of others as well as our own: *nobody* survives without help, and the beliefs of others—particularly those of the skillful outsider/observer—come through as objective reality even if it is not necessarily so. It was a long time before I realized that, for my own protection, the direct information telling I was getting from these professionals was partial and incomplete. They knew it when I did not.

8

CLAIMS AND PRIORITIES

Accidents will occur in the best regulated families.

—CHARLES DICKENS

Perhaps we were not even one of the "best regulated families." We have had our differences and our divorces, but, at the same time, we are a clear example of how infinitely elastic the umbilical cord can be without breaking and how the tics of shared experience can bind over distance and years. There are no part-time families. Maybe they are not always the conscious, central preoccupation of everyone's life, but what they have been and what they are structures and affects in every way all that happens throughout the life span. Family members— older or younger, same sex or opposite—are extensions of the self. What happens to one reverberates in each of the others, and that emotional fusion leads to even greater disruption when crises occur.

As a changing social invention, families are a specialized element in the natural system. It may not appear to be a permanent one, but, even when separation occurs, what has happened before continues to season what develops later. Clinical psychologists report that the adult who maintains contact with his or her family of origin is better equipped for continuing development than one who breaks away completely. Diminished involvement and parental acknowledgment of mutual autonomy take place even under conditions of continued contact. Families provide continuity.

Every family has its rituals, its patterns, its customs, and its styles of interaction, long established and used over and over again with mutual recognition. Their repetition underscores the expectations that each member has of the others. My childhood family was no different. My sister, Joan, reminded me that, when we went out in public with our parents (getting off a bus or going through a door, for example), Papa would conspicuously count us. (All those females! There were five of us when we were all together.) At home we had a time of day that was sacred to adulthood: the cocktail hour. From about 5:00 to 6:30 each evening before dinner this ritual took place. None of us had to be in the living room at that time, but, if we were, we could not read or talk to each other privately. We were expected to join in mutual, adult conversation—which was often clever and funny as well as informative—and we could have a stemmed glass of chilled lime juice diluted with water while our elders drank their martinis.

There was a ritual requirement connected with dinner time, too. We were expected to have read at least one newspaper article daily and to discuss it over the meal.

As with all families, our routines were learned, expected, and utilized as symbols of a membership system. The interaction of any "natural" group—biological or social—has to be considered as a system when the individuals belonging to it are well. They also have to be considered together—conjointly—when any one member becomes ill. But sickness changes the structure and processes within each group; integration patterns change. For example, families expand in crisis and retract when stability seems to be resuming. Structure evolves because the matching of family roles and patterns to the needs of its members is an absolute requirement for human development.

The appearance of a novel need causes temporary destabilization and then modification of these patterns. Illness causes disintegration of the social system, an alteration of conditions. And no formal interregnum appears between the old and the new. For a while it may all look terribly sloppy—with no clear rules and routines. Families under stress are extensively intertwined with each other, however—each person reactive to all. Family ties bind in adversity even more than in good fortune.

We are a never-ending feedback loop, stimuli for each other. It is never just an individual who is ill, but, rather, a part of a social organism. We are enmeshed in that social system, and, if that enmeshment is not broken and the perspective changed, it may prolong the illness instead of providing the support needed for mending. Why is this so? Because at the same time that the wings of the family fold in, each individual within their shelter needs desperately to utilize his or her relationship to the others as well as to the ill one. Needing each other, family members also need separation and access to each of their own private relationships with the sick one. However geographically separate its members were at the time of my illness, our family provided a context of mutual support. But the needs of the participants, their reactions to the situation, and their attempts to fulfill those needs, varied greatly. Our roles shifted in a disorder that seemed more idiosyncratic than purposeful at first.

What were those family roles and relationships? When I became ill, I was separated from my siblings by three thousand miles and from my parents by some five hundred. Helen, a mycologist and the older of my still-living sisters, was at home in Rochester, New York, then. (Her husband, Wolf Vishniac, had been killed on a NASA expedition in Antarctica the previous year.) As the wife of James MacGregor Burns, the historian, my sister Joan lived in the Berkshire mountain country in western Massachusetts. My parents had retired from Harvard University and had the company of an aunt close by who had been their life-long intimate. I was divorced from Allan, who had briefly been the stepfather of my three young adult children, but almost all of us were still good friends.

Because my father and Aunt Marty wanted to say good-by to me in person, they left my mother under the authority of hospital care and that of my quickly summoned sister and came to Los Angeles. In that double crisis my father traded "husbanding" for "fathering," mourned so deeply in anticpation of my death that, at my bedside, he did not see any index of hope, even the flutter of an eyelid (reported by his granddaughter), which might have been taken to mean that consciousness was emerging at last. He had been through one daughter's death in maturity, and here was another dying. Things were happening out of order. To avoid the pain of suspense, of struggle with an unresolved situation, and the agony of trying to sustain hope, I think that he gave up and accepted my death as inevitable, actual, final.

I think now that there may have been another factor affecting my father's failure to continue to hope: he is a scientist. He is a scientist with a life-long belief in scientific methodology and the validity of the knowledge derived from it. Much of medical care is applied science. It is based on systematic, controlled testing and recording. The physicians attending me were trained in this applied science and, when they expressed their belief that I was dying, he believed them.

When I finally went home from the hospital, my oldest child, too, took on the parental role. I had lost the freedom of choice that comes with maturity, but, for a long time, I did not rebel. I did what I was told to do. When I finally did become a disobedient dependent, I still needed what I was rejecting. Rejection and need had become inseparable. *I could not do without others, and I did not want them because to want their help, to need them, was incontestable evidence of my own incapability.* The limits of my reality were being laid down by others—not out of pure love for me (altruism) or the need to feel powerful in this situation (egotism) on their parts, but a combination of the two. I felt restricted.

The relationship with Jim and Joan Burns changed, too. Jim I had met several times, but I did not know him well at all. Joan was the only sister with whom I had lived for more than two years while we were growing up. During the summer of 1975 —eight months after I had come home from the hospital—our closeness, while diluted by space, time, and other emotional commitments, brought her to invite me to cross the country and go with them on their annual vacation to Barn House.

Founded many years ago on Martha Vineyard, Barn House was a cooperative at Chilmark with an annual membership fee and reserved space for families who returned year after year alone or with friends. Like the occupants of hotels, visitors paid a daily rate for the time they were there. The cook and a choreboy who washed the dishes were hired, but the temporary occupants dried them and were expected generally to contribute some labor to the upkeep of the place. (Jim trimmed back overenthusiastic shrubbery on the grounds; Joan, when she had to, went grocery shopping. Everyone was expected to maintain his or her own living quarters.) Private cabins—so-called "coops"—clustered at some distance around an enormous remodeled barn with a stone fireplace, space for convivial dinners, and an area ideal for lively after-dinner talk.

While I was there, Roger Baldwin, the ancient founder of the American Civil Liberties Union, spun out historical tales of the social life of the nation and his own, combined. Professionally, we summer visitors came from a variety of worlds.

Joan told me recently that Warren Chappell, illustrator, book designer, and member of Barn House, had been there with his wife during my stay. He had commented to her on what an "aesthetic object" I was, saying that I had a kind of ethereal quality. Extreme thinness combined with delicate coloration. I had begun to gain weight by that time, but I was still spare-boned, still losing my way if I wandered three yards from the door of the cabin without companionship. Joan took my arm; Jim took my arm—wherever we went. (At home in Santa Monica once out of sight of my apartment building I could not find my way home. Over and over as I walked I got directions to the grocery story I had been patronizing for five years. Once there, little Marty picked me and the groceries up. I never learned to take it for granted that I needed help in finding direction, but I got used to asking.)

I remember the nudists' beach on Martha's Vineyard, where naked sunbathers sometimes protected themselves from the inquisitive stares of passerbys by burying themselves in the sand the way that alligators do in water. I remember the churning Atlantic, thinking of my own neighborhood ocean in California and recognizing why mine was called the "Pacific." We walked to Quiet Pond (off Noisy Beach), which led to Menemsha Pond, a lake of fresh, clear water so slightly separated by sand banks from the tides that it seemed impossible for it to be free from salt.

I lay down on those still waters as if they had been a solid mattress beneath me and I were dreamlessly afloat in my sleep. Completely bouyant, sublimely relaxed, I drifted to the actual border of sleep, slipped beyond it briefly and returned, slipped beyond it and returned over and over again. Not far from me Jim swam; Joan watched anxiously from the shore. Back on the sand I tried to stay on my feet since, once down, getting up again was real labor, even with a cane—first to my knees and then to whatever nearby supports I could find, usually available arms.

One day, as we were walking back from the beach, Jim began to talk about the project he was working on at that time—a psychosocial, historical study of moral leadership in the political world. Some years before my illness I had become interested in the development of morality over the life span and especially in the studies done by two psychologists, Jean Piaget in Europe and Lawrence Kohlberg in the United States. I had published some articles which, later, when I discovered his interest in the field, I had discussed with Jim, and there, in the sweet, late afternoon air, he suggested that I could be helpful to him in his current work. To me, at the time the suggestion was laughable, *absolutely* unbelievable.

What could my cooperation, my resources contribute to his study when I could not control either my muscles or my mind? He insisted, and finally I agreed, feeling foolishly inadequate and not taking him seriously. I was sure that he was only being nice to me, insisting that I was still an intelligent, knowledgeable academic because he was "family" then and because I needed as much support in building my self-esteem and sense of personal adequacy as caring friends and relatives could afford to give.

Given my state of intellectual disarray, the outcome of this collaboration could not have been better. I could not read, research, or write anything new, so I dug into my files and supplied Jim with references and papers written earlier. I commented in laborious, repetitious—at least so it seemed to me —writing on what he wrote, and, again separated from much of family and all of my professional world, I greatly enjoyed his ruminative telephone calls across the continent. He was a night worker and, by East Coast time, often phoned well after midnight there. Personal warmth flowed through the mail service and the telephone wires. I was forced to try to move beyond the narrow domesticity of exercise and self-examination, to turn my thinking (such as it was) to the outer world, the work of others, and to practice communication—especially difficult when I could not use body language to span the gaps created by the loss of words and memory.

Researchers have found a high degree of association between health changes and family-life-cycle events, including the illness or death of other members of the family. Some months into my long convalescence my older daughter, Marty, on whom I was still completely dependent, was beset with a series of persistent symptoms which never seemed to disappear or to be treatable. She went into the hospital for a week of testing. Minor problems were located but nothing that could really explain her difficulties. Fortunately, in time she got better.

A group of scientists has tried to find out whether the physical illness of parents affects the measurable intelligence quotient of their children. It did not make any difference whether the sick parent was the father or the mother; the IQ of the child living at home did not change. However, even if *illness* of a parent did not have any effect, *hospitalization* did. When the mother was the one put into the hospital, IQ was temporarily lowered. When the father was hospitalized, no effect was evident, probably because to a child at a young age his absence was not experienced as so threatening as the mother's.

Studies like that one bear out what we all learn in the course of life—through fiction, if not through personal experience— that fear gets in the way of the thinking process, that it is crippling even if it is not for oneself but for a loved one.

Membership in a family is not like that in a club; it is not subject to expiration, and the dues are not fixed. Members may seek out each other because they want to use each other's knowledge, skills, or contacts, but, more important, they provide attachment, caring, and loyalty for each other. In spite of this, there is *never* a time when the needs of any single member are *completely* met. And help for developmental needs is provided only when survival ones have been adequately fulfilled.

Can family members continue to react positively and openly to each other when they are each swimming desperately in a sea of emotional intensity? Uncertainty made those in my family seek support from each other at the same time they were so busy dealing with their own feelings that the needs of others seemed intrusive. Worrying about others gets in the way of focus on the self. And at such a time every misunderstanding is exaggerated into rejection and defiance or neglect. While I was still in the coma in the hospital, my children and Allan planned a joint dinner in my apartment for all the relatives visiting at that time. My aunt incited a good deal of pain and resentment when she rejected the invitation to my father and herself by saying, "We're not in the mood for a party!" Nobody was putting on a party; they were looking for the nourishment of shared company and food in a way of coping with disaster and death which has occurred in many different cultures over millennia.

The clearest example of differences in coping styles and the difficulties of drawing on each other for mutual support in mutual crisis came from my three children. Close in age (Bethany, the youngest, was twenty years old—they were all born within three years of each other), they were individuals, distinctive and idiosyncratic. Separate egos, separate personalities going about the business of problem solving, each for him- or herself. But each of their choices affected those of other members of the family.

Marty, the oldest at twenty-three, took on the responsibilities of family head and tried hard to exert some kind of control over my custody and care, over household management, and over the behavior of her brother and sister. Trying to hold the situation together, she led by indirection, working, for example, with the others on a schedule of shared, hospital attendance, drawing them into conversation, into talks without confrontation, to try to help all of them make order out of the abiding emotional chaos they were caught in. But her attempts at leading or working with her siblings were not all successful. Leaders have to be chosen by their followers, and sometimes they interpreted those advances as manifestations of a need for dominance and would have none of them. Over the long period of my convalescence she was much more willing than either of the other two to spend time with me on errands, cleaning, and meal preparation, response to my mail, and all the miscellaneous tasks of low-key living in the apartment retreat. Even after she moved away, she called me daily to get a progress report and to find out whether there was something she could do or get for me.

There was nothing swarmy about any of my children. They did not flatter or attempt to ingratiate themselves with me or with other family members. Nor were their critical powers inhibited by my own definition of my capacities. They observed and decided for themselves, sometimes for very different reasons and arriving at very different conclusions. Marty talked to the nurses and doctors, and she believed what she was told. Garth heard many of the same frightening, negative statements and reacted by radical avoidance—first by insisting that there was nothing anyone could do about it and so why worry, then by denial that anything serious or lasting was wrong with me, and, finally, by withdrawal into himself, away from anyone who might make unbearable demands upon him by insisting that he face a reality that he refused to recognize.

Because Bethany had been with me during the onset of my

illness, she had had all the responsibility of finding adequate medical care for me. For the first weeks, until others were told and came, she was completely alone at these tasks, and, although crippled by anxiety, she did what had to be done. As time went by and routine bills began to come in, she was sure that none of them had to be paid by her because I would soon be home to pay them myself. She was the co-signer on my checking account although she had never used it. Later, when Marty had come from the East, Bethany relinquished her responsibilities to her sister, assuming that she and their grandfather would pay the bills. Then she went ahead and made plans for the resumption of her own life—school and travel—while denying that none of it might be possible with my income ending and huge medical expenses pending. She was foolheartedly, defensively denying all the fatal expectations and conclusions of authority, and one day, in a salving, defiant act of pretense, she went out to the stores and spent one hundred fifty dollars on designer jeans and a top for herself—something she had never been allowed to do. (Nor had anyone else in the family—adult or child.)

As many of us do when we suddenly become aware of the limits of the control we have over our lives, she was overwhelmed by her sense of lovelessness, abandonment, and isolation—from others as well as from me, since I was so thoroughly changed. Fear and loss of stability sent her floundering, adrift. But she still identified with me, and, in a crippling series of role-modeling acts, she sought out comparable experiences—experiences that were not disease-producing but that were still seriously health- or life-threatening just the same.

I can write about this now because it did not end in disaster as it might have. We have all emerged from the fire cleansed. The dangerous, pseudoprotective behavior of that time has been developed into new ways of living; the roots of sound values are alive and growing, all the more cherished because their existence was threatened in that dark past. Progress often looks like destruction, but, unless previous pathways are blocked or ruined, why should new ones be sought or used?

Today, Marty is finishing school at the University of California at Los Angeles; Garth has become a computer engineer and has found an important feminine adjunct to his life; Bethany graduated with honors from the University of California at Berkeley two years ago and is a full-time feature writer for the *Oakland Tribune*. Her assignments and her travels have inner dimensions as well as outer ones. All three are in touch with each other as well as themselves, for, like me, they have learned that self-sufficiency is an evanescent property, subject to attack by every vicissitude of life. And family claims and priorities are lasting and real. Community—whether within the enduring, biological family or beyond it—provides more than support. It supplies a balm for mending the striving spirit.

9

GOD'S PLACE

Homo semper aliud, Fortuna aliud cognitat
("Man proposes, God disposes").

For some months my lack of self-consciousness protected me from realizing who I had become. When I searched for an illusive word or a memory, when I stood up and dizziness muddied my eyes and rang in my ears, when I collided with solid, invisible barriers close on the right side of my body or tripped over nothing and fell, fell, fell over and over and over again, I groped, shifted, or got up and went on. Every step and every moment lived meant coping on an ad hoc basis. For a long time I had no past and no plans, not even for an *hour* later. When I made them, I forgot them until they reappeared arbitrarily some time in the future. Or I wrote them down and misplaced the paper with the message on it.

I did not worry about understanding. Meaning eluded me completely. I did not miss it; I was not searching for it. But then I began to get better, and the questions began to arise—questions of meaning and purpose.

Like two of my sisters, I had been raised a Unitarian—part of a religious group to whose faith people are more often converted than they are born. My father's parents themselves had moved from the Baptist Church to a Unitarian one, and so, in due course, I became a third-generation member in the beautiful, strong buildings in Washington, D.C., and in Manhattan. Members of this religious congregation, now united with the Universalists as the Unitarian Universalist Association, have very few beliefs in common. The church I joined in New York, All Souls, had a simple statement of purpose:

> In the freedom of truth and in the spirit of Jesus, we unite for the worship of God and the service of man.

For me, the role of the son, Jesus, in the heavenly hierarchy has never been in doubt: he is an intensely admirable hero, a mortal, and a martyr, no god. But the definition of the father is much more ambiguous. Members of the congregation differ widely (and often noisily) in their imagery of the powers ascribed to God. Many deny the concept of deity altogether. How I sounded off in this cacophony before my illness, I have no idea. Scholars in the Middle Ages repeatedly affirmed that they believed in a Supreme Being *because* it was absurd *("Credo quia absurdum est")* or *even* if it were unreasonable *("Credo nisi absurdum est")* to do so. Such a deity could only be recognized and worshiped by blind faith; it could never be reached solely through the intellectual patterns of philosophers or theology students.

There are reasons for belief in a general God, but there can be times when I need some for accepting a particular one. So do many others, as Mortimer Adler has described in his book *How to Think about God: A Guide for the Twentieth-Century Pagan.* * We have to posit the existence of a god—a sapient, all-powerful being—in order to explain the *actual* existence

*(New York: Macmillan, 1980).

here and now of a merely *possible* cosmos. Why did it all come to exist? Why does it continue? The word *God* appears in slightly varying forms in all Teutonic languages and is believed to derive from a Sanskrit root, *ghu*, which means "to worship." This word *God* is in no way connected with the word *good*. And anyone who has read the Old Testament would have trouble thinking of that God as inevitably moral or virtuous in any way approaching modern definition.

The "divinity that shapes our ends, rough-hew them how we will" (as the Prince of Denmark described it) has a variety of attributes, depending on who is doing the describing. Its nature is to be known as something within us that is other than ourselves and something within the universe that is not separate, individual pieces but something valuable and indivisible, eternal and ineluctable. The God I hope for is the solitary force occupying a transcendent realm, whose self is loving, compassionate, beneficent, and who radiates a supernatural beauty and health whose influence is enjoyed—not endured—by all. But this is a vision that I have found to have little basis in reality.

Mending, I became depressed because I believed myself defeated by a being capricious, illogical, all-powerful, and more than a little petty and malevolent. Or was I defeated by my *belief* in that being and not the being itself? I do not know. At any rate, I became tuned out and stricken with despair and a sense of impotence. There is nothing flagitious in depression, but one can be ashamed of oneself for feeling that way and letting it affect what one does and thinks. The problem is that the *first* time something awful happens there is no way of knowing that this has happened before and has been coped with and so could be dealt with again whenever it recurs. I had to decide what was being fought, what could be done about it, and how. Under these circumstances even teleology was of no help; what was the use of believing that purpose and design exist in nature if all the planned routes seem dangerous and dead-ended? Such purpose has to be for good if you are to bear to believe in it and in design and work as the way to achieve it.

So I declared myself recusant—obstinately refusing to submit to those mysterious, negative forces suddenly centered on me. But then those forces, those external powers, were not complying with that role definition! Whatever had made me ill was not granting me the authority to make myself well; autonomy was a myth, I realized in panic as I began to be able to assess my situation. Chance and impotence were overwhelming me. I could have given up and accepted what was happening to me as a fitting punishment for earlier sins, long forgotten and perhaps never acknowledged. I did neither although I did withdraw, go into hiding in my limited space and hope that the Great Scan would pass me by after this one mighty whack!

I sought anonymity and obscurity, but not everyone defends him- or herself in the same way. For example, one of the stroke victims I read about commented that, after his illness, he had joined the Episcopal Church. He did that because he felt better believing that there was a "Power that is not as vulnerable as Man." Going to church cauterized what had happened to him as it could not have done for me because belief in an invulnerable power for *evil* or for *mischief* is no help at all!

In the eighteenth century William Cowper wrote about the need to see beyond the terrifying façade to the force that would come to man's aid:

> God moves in a mysterious way
> His wonders to perform;
> He plants his footsteps in the sea,
> And rides upon the storm . . .

Judge not the Lord by feeble sense,
But trust him for his grace;
Behind a frowning providence
He hides a smiling face.

But the "frowning providence" has a reality. I believe the line found in the book of Acts in the Bible: "God is no respecter of persons." And for the poet, Robert Browning, to write with joyful hope "God's in his heaven—All's right with the world!" seems to me to be the short-sighted hyperbole of a happy man. Can I believe such a thing when that global generalization does not correspond at all to the subjective reality of my everyday life? Can I transcend my ordinary perceptions of this material world, connect my consciousness with stereotypic heavenly regions? If I could, a *loving* God might become a self-evident reality and not a matter of struggling for belief and definition at all.

Possibility alone is not sufficient cause for the existence of anything, even God. There must be an exnihilating cause for any actualization, *any* coming to be. Then, too, there is a world of difference between believing in God as a beneficent power, confiding and hoping in him or her, and just believing that he or she exists. His or her existence may be indisputable, but divine moral goodness, perfection, even justice and mercy or loving benevolence toward mortal creatures are more than a little questionable. Existence alone does not entitle God to these attributes, and there is no rational necessity for thinking of God this way, for little evidence supports such thought. Divine inscrutability need not be accompanied by superabundant goodness; God's actions are often unjustifiable by any standard acceptable to contemporary civilization.

Adler put it very clearly:

To acknowledge God's omnipotence and omniscience, as we
must, is to acknowledge that he knows and understands us
better than we understand ourselves, that nothing about us is
hidden from him and that, within the bounds of possibility, he
can do with us as he wills. However, to acknowledge this is not
to be assured that God is concerned with our conduct or cares
what happens to us.*

Perhaps the difficulty is that we have invented an an-
thropomorphic God, one made in our own image, and so we
try to describe him as we would other humans, rather than
analogically. The attempt fails because what comes through is
a petty, not a magnificent, image. God is the only uncaused
cause, the only being whose existence did not derive from
someone or something else. Only he or she is *ex nihilo*, supernatural, and with the power to accomplish exnihilation and
annihilation himself or herself. As the Supreme Being, he or
she has created the cosmos out of nothing, just as he or she is
responsible for its preservation, the end of the universe, or its
everlasting existence. God is self-derived and self-originated; he
or she has what the philosophers call "aseity"—being derived
from, through, and in oneself and not from any other source.

"I am who (that) I am," God told Moses, declaring his
singularity as the meeting was reported in the Old Testament.
Since he has in himself a sufficient reason for his own existence,
he must also have the power of self-definition, design, and
construction. Creation and healing may be God's work as he
sees it and chooses, but, if so, he is also smiter and destroyer.
Who or what was responsible for my becoming sick? And who
beat the illness in this complicated battle? Did the doctors save
my life? Was it the natural power of their medicine that did

*Ibid., p. 167.

it, or the collaborative efforts of myself, those who love me, and the doctors? And God? It is easy to thank God for what seems like an inexplicable miracle, but why is it equally easy to forget that, if the All Powerful was responsible for the healing, he or she must have also been responsible for the sickness in the first place?

> Ah! must—
> Designer infinite!
> Ah! must Thou char the wood ere Thou canst
> limn with it?

The mystic Francis Thompson's God damaged the wood in order to use the altered material as a tool. Was I, too, chosen as a means and injured in order to implement some purpose? Or was it all aleatory—my illness and recovery? All unpredictable chance? The whimsy of nature or a capricious God who could not make up his mind what to do with me?

Sometimes I believe that if there had not been counterdemands for my presence—the human ones of that vigilant family and friends—I would have slipped away even under those half-hearted, lackadaisical pressures. The bonds of love are tight ones, elastic but unbreakable. There was something there that I could not evade, invisible, enduring demands that the elusive, evaporating spirit could not escape. As Seneca wrote long ago, exits are everywhere. Had I wanted to die, I would have. But who could be so loved and wanted and give up? They would not let me separate myself. Suicide, according to Alvarez,* is an outcome of "the final unbearable illumination that God is not good," a state of mind he compares to the *psychic numbness* described by Robert Jay Lifton. The active choice

---

*Alfred Alvarez, *The Savage God: A Study of Suicide* (New York: Bantam, 1971).

for death is an attempt to force God to acknowledge the existence of the person and that person's ability to choose for him- or herself.

Illness has shown me the triviality of my single life; God had made clear its inconsequentiality to him or her. (One more weed among so many others!) It was only mortals who defined it as valuable, beloved, needed. And so I did not want God to acknowledge my existence any further or even to notice it. I wanted him or her to permit me to find my own way, to insist upon it by absenting himself or herself from my life. I wanted to reclaim my right to choice.

I believe in this God, but not with certitude, not beyond a reasonable doubt. The unsettled question for me now is not really whether God exists but, rather, in what form and how arbitrarily, how reasonably. Perhaps now the task is not really to find answers but to learn how to live with the questions. Pain and misfortune are always unanswered questions. They always hunger for meaning. To suffer either of them is to ask: What do they mean? Am I being punished? If I am, there must be some cause; I must be guilty. I must have done something to have earned this punishment. I think that I have probably always been a painstaking person, taking pains to try to do things well. We use these expressions—*painstaking* and *taking pains*—to mean "methodical," "full of care," not to mean "hurtful," but there is a deeply held relationship as old as Rome in the ancient Latin. The word *poena* meant not just "pain," but also "punishment." Pain arrived as a punishment. The two concepts were inseparable.

Suffering may lead to insight but not to more accurate outsight. In either case, pain of the spirit or the flesh can be more easily borne than neutrality or the absence of feeling. It can speak to us directly and be heard as a symptom of life.

Does religion only have to do with occasions of sorrow and suffering, when we need all the patience and forbearance we can muster? Is it only a means of keeping me—and others— from breaking under the impact of calamity? Literally, the word *religion* means "that which reconnects." If by the study and practice of religion is meant the discovery of a unified inner dimension of being, the illumination of immediate, nondiscursive knowledge about myself and my relationship to all else, then the use of the word *religion* makes sense. But if it means only a network of established *social* practices, it makes no sense at all—especially when some versions of Heaven and Hell seem to be abstract and rather silly adaptations of life on earth. Heaven and Hell *do* exist in *this* world, but blame is not assigned arbitrarily by rational people, and both good intentions and ignorance may let people off the hook. That has not always been so in the history of the gods.

A classic example of heavenly retribution is told in *Oedipus Rex*, the first play of Sophocles' trilogy. The inhumane, unavoidable force of divine power is enacted against the king, who has, unknowingly, erred. He knows the laws against patricide and incest and has not deliberately broken them. His excuse— and it is a legitimate one—is not ignorance of the law but, more simply, not knowing what he has done or what he was doing while he was doing it—the meaning attached to his actions. He has killed his father and married his mother without knowing the identity of either of them. By drought, famine, and infertility, the gods have punished the people of Thebes for their ruler's acts, yet these very gods are the ones who have set up his immorality and thereby manufactured his misfortunes and those of his subjects. Why should a person inflict reprisals on himself for acts that he has done without knowledge of what his choice for them truly means? He did not *choose* to do these dreadful deeds, but he is so repelled by the self-discovery of them that he mutilates himself by putting out his eyes. (There is a parallel here with the Roman Catholic practice in which the person must recognize and acknowledge his sin before he can do penance as a means of attaining forgiveness.)

By blaming himself, or at least accepting responsiblity, Oedipus has taken the blame off the malicious, petty immortals who have tricked him into folly. But if he did not know what he was doing while he was doing it, how could he have been blamed or even been held responsible for the outcome of his actions? The gods have determined what has happened to him, and, insofar as they have the power to do that, he has none to resist them. All that can save him is consciousness of his inabilities and, therefore, the limits of that responsibility. Because he does not have that, he is doomed to suffer. Oedipus has been trapped in the assumptions of his time and culture.

Whether the route is through science or religion, all the ways of understanding reality require investment in their assumptions. We make our reality by what we are willing to accept. And many of us are trapped by our own need for belief in miracles and mystery: we have faith in faith for its own sake. Dostoevsky wrote that "the only answer to a mystery is another mystery," and that is the way that many of us like it. Faith is a handrail. Freya Stark goes even further to say that she believes a definition of happiness would be awareness that there is something of the unknown in our pattern of life. Anything finished or consummated palls because the unknown has ceased to surround it; the vista of discovery or exploration and not completion is what keeps us active and aware, seeking and, therefore, happy.

Not long ago I read a review of a book written by a rabbi who had interviewed hundreds of survivors from the World

War II concentration camps.* What he reported was similar to what I had found within myself: God is not *necessarily* sought in extremity; faith is by no means spontaneous. Doubt, disappointment, and distrust are daily fare. If God is not trustworthy and his motives positive and rational, he or she is avoided as more aggravation than help. More survivors had *abandoned* their belief in God's ability and willingness to help than had turned to religion for solace or explanation. If evil exists, then it was created—and the creator of all is responsible for it.

I have taken an existential approach, trying to work through this experience for myself, to understand it and to find meaning in it. But my existentialism is not the whole cloth of Sartre's despairing manufacture, emphasizing atheism along with alienation, human aloneness, individuality, and self-reliance. Alone, individual, my own decision maker I may be and, for many reasons, need to be, but I do not depend on myself alone. Nor, for all the sense of growing strength in my distinctive self, will I be alienated from others. I have learned more about them because I know more about myself. "I am a part of all that I have seen," Tennyson's Ulysses knew at the end of his travels, and so am I, although still hoping there are more journeys ahead.

I have made my own compromise between the extreme of existentialism and its opposite philosophical pole: the transcendental phenomenology and mysticism of writers such as Marcel, who perceive human life as supported by a web of belief in God and by mutual communion and participation. Neither view seems to me to be true by itself or to be absolutely true.

*Philip Friedman, *Roads to Extinction: Essays on the Holocaust* (Philadelphia: Jewish Publication Society of America, 1981).

Together they can be seen as a dialectic description of Being, co-existing in the vast range of consciousness. If Niels Bohr, the physicist, could find comfortable reality in both quantum mechanics and Newtonian physics and build a principle of complementarity or correspondence, then why should I find it difficult to utilize two opposing understandings of biological nature? *Any* belief that is held without possibility of modification or shift is an inert one, no longer dynamic and applicable.

But order is needed—and a sense of power, however limited. The worst anxiety arises when events are felt to be completely random, without pattern, design, or control. I can live without certitude but not without belief in my ability to influence what happens to me and not without hope or meaning, however complicated that is. Would a life without suffering be one without meaning? It would certainly be an unimaginable one. Do we need to suffer in order to be human and separate, to learn to overcome the experience of finitude? Some contemporary philosophers seem to believe so. Their abstractions on the subject act as intellectual stimuli, but they do not solve the specific problems of personal existence. If I can escape death or suffering only by identifying myself with the cosmic stream of consciousness, then I have so completely lost my sense of the person I am as an individual that the problem is not solved. The most important choice is not between continuity and disjunction, between life and death, but between authentic or inauthentic life as experienced by the single person, each of us alone.

The purpose of life is to discover the meaning of existence —existence that includes inevitable disease and loss and pain, not as *all* there is but certainly as a part of the whole plan. Can *being* be good if it includes evil of these sorts, as well as one that is felt all the more strongly because it originates in *human* decisions and acts? Can we make use of evil that is seen to be part of a larger design, a pattern of ultimate good that bounds and, therefore, controls it? What kind of freedom do I have within that design? If I am free to design for myself in any proportion, then I am responsible for my decision making, and a sense of responsibility, acted upon, must lead to humility. This is no petty moralism but, rather, the voice of the grim realist speaking. Each day presents situational double binds in which one must choose the lesser of evils, without either of them being a good. There is no way to do what is right, to get *all* your "druthers"; there is only a way to reconcile oneself with what is possible and what is not at any given moment or place. And what I choose has to do with me, with who *I* am, as value is always received in reference to a particular person and is not objective, absolute, or independent.

Thinking reasonably may get in the way of faith in anything that does not have clear empirical support, but thinking *by itself* will not get to the truth of anything either. Some things that I do not understand, that I cannot reason out, I still have learned to accept. (The awakening moment, breath upon one's cheek, mutual contact in a glance, the structure of growing things, the emanations of love across distance, dark and sleep . . .) Life can be meaningful without a trustworthy God just because reality is multidimensional, neither groundless nor aimless nor obvious. I have an enduring resistance to the Christian acceptance of God's will. Must I be utterly determined by eternal forces? I *do not* believe it, and I *will not* believe it!

"God help us!" The wrenching cry is rarely heard; response to it is arbitrary. Are there limitations on that eternal power? Does he or she suffer from impotence after all? From the misery he or she or his or her *alter ego*, the Devil, inflicts or does not end when it is inflicted by others? Can such a God be a refuge or a source or even a proper antagonist—not a trivial one or a fluke actor into mischief because he or she is bored, not very bright, and indifferent? Along with the rest of us I say "God willing" when I am orally knocking on wood, but the use of this Americanized *como Dio vuole* is not even superstition; it is empty routine and cultural pattern. The prayerful belief "Thy Will be Done, Lord" can easily be seen as a real sloughing of personal responsibility for trying.

One can indict divine silence, indifference, ambiguity, or even vindictiveness, but in fact it is *human* behavior and not that divine providence which is daily tested. And it is my self which must be the source of aspiration or regeneration. Writing in "The Accident," Elie Wiesel tells the story of a narrator who asks the doctor who has just operated on him whether he believes in God. "Yes," the doctor answered. "But not in the operating room. There I only count on myself." That is keeping the God-self relationship in proper proportion!

10

TRIAL AND ERROR

This is *my* way; where is yours?—Thus I
answered those who asked me "the way." For
the way—that does not exist.
> —Friedrick Wilhelm Nietzsche

In the beginning of the second year of my recuperation I was
beginning to fight the need to get permission from my body
to do certain things. I had enough belief in my balance to try
to ride my daughter's bicycle in the great sheltered garage
under my apartment building, when most of the occupants had
driven off to work. Holding the handle bars with one hand and
the seat behind me with the other, a friend ran alongside to
get me started, then freed me and stepped back. I sailed off,
wobbling dangerously but still upright until I got to the turning
point—a choice of uphill or two broad columns supporting the
roof—where I deliberately fell off to keep it from happening
accidentally. We went down to the open parking lots by the
ocean and tried again. I gained maximally in confidence and
minimally in skill. Learning to ride a two-wheeler, years before,
by no means must have been so difficult; in adolescence I must
have gotten on the bike and started off. I had ridden through
eastern mountains, hosteling with friends.

In relearning, I found my rising confidence my undoing: in a few weeks I set off on the twenty-five-mile cement bike path with a friend elegantly riding his trim ten-speed along the beach beside me. It was a perfect day, the air clear, the nearby waters shiny with vitality. Concentrating, I was doing well, keeping the borrowed machine moving smoothly beneath me. But then my companion spoke. I did not hear what he had said, and I turned my head toward him to see it being said again. Disaster! We had reached a part of Venice where the bike path is bounded by a low concrete wall on the sea side, and the bike and I went into it, almost over it. A six-inch gash in one leg was pouring out blood. I felt sick; my friend was visibly shaken, and another bicyclist offered his huge neckerchief to staunch the flow. With considerable obstinacy, silent, with vision fixed straight ahead, I rode home that day, but, so far, I have not tried again. (At our last meeting my doctor, who never forbade me anything, suggested that I should not, that my balance will never be trustworthy.)

I did get back to biking, though, in another way. Some days Marty and I went for miles along the sands, sharing a bicycle built for two. We did this a number of times before she admitted that the joy and relaxation I felt were not shared by her. She was much too aware of my unpredictable weight shifts in the rear seat, much too unsure she could control the machine for herself as well as for me. We gave up the venture.

In the spring of 1976 I began to learn to drive again. Generous as always with her time, Marty had been taking me on errands, making sure that I got there and back and, when I was getting my repeated medical checkups, that she had heard and recorded what report was made and advice given to me. (I was prone not to hear and, even more, not to remember and apply. In this way I was still the child and she the mother.) As my social investment in the city beyond my apartment increased,

I took the bus more and more. The time lost was not important to me then. My Audi sat for months with no more life stirring than a random short excursion or its motor run for a lengthy warmup while the car remained immobile. Out of practice, I still felt confident; I had been a good driver and a relaxed, alert one. (At least, so I believe.) As my energy returned, I expected old motor patterns and reflexes to emerge in short order.

As usual, I was wrong, of course. Past competence in this, as in every field of knowledge, was not to be revived so easily. What I had done automatically—keeping track of traffic ahead, behind, to the side—had to be done as a conscious, continued effort. Even with my new glasses and the range-expander patch on the right lens, I had a difficult time figuring distance. Three times—perfectly sure that I was clear of it— I scraped the right rear car door on the post at the foot of my parking space. I had to learn how to concentrate ceaselessly— no looking at the scenery and no talking! I was all over the road —a menace—and I knew it. But I was determined to regain my mobility and the power it represented.

When Eve picked a forbidden apple, what began that day was an important virtue called *disobedience.* My daughter's disapproval incited stealth. (You will remember that I was still a "maturing adolescent!") But she was well aware of what I was up to, and when she reached the end of her endurance, Marty enlisted a friend who sat beside me, totally without comment, simply ordering, "Turn left." "Pass the blue car." "Stop." I responded equally unemotionally, and, in time, it worked. I learned, although I will never again be the automatically good driver that I believe I once was.

The neutrality of my instructor was a help. She was not denying my limitations, only insisting that I test them. Sometimes it is a good thing that the whole do not believe in the partial, the strong in the weak, or the seeing in the blind. The capacity to share such experience has to be learned. When it is not, the disabled may feel very painfully the doubt and lack of faith with which their personal experience is received. Any disability has its own function. It has to be understood as an altered state of perception, not as a difficiency that must be compensated for at any price. Close your eyes if you want to see; be still if you want to walk; put your hands over your ears if you want to hear. These are valid ways of making contact, of becoming aware.

None of the senses, none of the body's capabilities, exists alone. They are interdependent. My illness changed my ways of perceiving, of receiving information, but it did not extinguish them.

Even when I had regained considerable facility at observing and reacting, I realized that I was stuck with the need for perpetual vigilance in a way I had never anticipated before. I have to be unceasingly *attentive*. Driving is only one example of this, one which became apparent in the fall of 1976, when I was going one day a week down to Irvine to teach a class at the university there. Driving in consistent freeway traffic at sixty miles per hour (five miles an hour past the legal limit but in a uniform crowd doing the same thing), I was listening to my favorite classical-music radio station as I went. Casually, I lifted my eyes to the mirror, assuming nothing, expecting nothing.

But something was there: blinking headlights in the mid-morning and (as I promptly turned the radio off) a screeching police siren. When he came over to my stopped car, the driver was cordial enough; he had expected to find me drunk or drugged, told me he had been behind me for five miles, flashing the pull-over signals all the way, before he turned on the siren. No, I had simply not known he was there. I took the ticket with some chagrin—as a bitter reminder of my sensory and attention limitations—and, to this day, I do not know if, indeed, I have relearned or if it has been the physical mending that has reoriented time and space for me. I have learned caution, too, and you need not move a safe lane or two away as the neat grey car, scarred on one side, approaches.

In the early second spring of my recovery, I was beginning to think seriously about the possibility of going back to work. If I could not do academic work anymore, then I would have to do another kind—to learn another occupation. I had taken over my own financial affairs by then and was very much aware that my textbook royalties were bound to run out in time. In how *much* time I had no way of knowing. Unexpectedly, I got a phone call from Simon Fraser University in British Columbia. A summer program on humanistic education with guest speakers from other parts of Canada, England, and the United States was being set up. One of my colleagues had been invited, could not go, and had suggested that I be asked in his place.

That was George Brown at the University of California at Santa Barbara, who, for some years, had been preparing educators to teach confluent education—education of both intellect and affect, both thinking and feeling capacities of humankind. George knew that I had been ill; but I had not seen him since I had gotten out of the hospital, and he had no idea of my current condition. Neither did the caller who was following through on the recommendation. Once I learned that there would be three public lectures (which I could write out beforehand, putting together materials already published, and deliver by reading) and a weekly three-hour seminar for a small group of graduate students, I wanted very much to accept. It seemed to me that it was time for another try.

My doctor disagreed. He did not believe that I had either the stamina or the necessary verbal and other intellectual capabilities to do a professional job at that time. He discouraged me from going, but I would not listen. I wanted both the money and the chance to test myself and—I hoped—to succeed once again in academic life.

I went, but it was a skinny victory, gathered from undemanding students and friendly strangers who did not know how much I had lost and who seemed to me incredibly nonjudgmental. Among those who were visiting there, too, I met John McLeish, Edmund Sullivan, and Jonathan Kozol, who had raised his usual popular following. In my customary pattern since illness, I did not recognize Ed, with whom I had served on a professional panel several years before. McLeish and his wife were most kind to me, and it was he who, taking on a new post at the University of Victoria, brought me there the following summer.

By fall, on short notice, I was asked if I wanted to teach a course at the University of California of Irvine, where many people still remembered my dramatic disappearance several years before when my illness struck. The summer had emboldened me; I took on a course. It was a disastrous and fortunately brief attempt at *tour de force*. I was teaching undergraduates, who were nervous about grades and even more so about unconventional teaching styles. Since leaving Berkeley, I had not taught either undergraduates or lecture courses, but that was not the reason I structured the class the way I did. With fixed concentration, I was beginning to read again by then, but I still could not recall information on demand. Even with notes, lecturing was impossible. I assigned area studies within the course to small groups and organized the class sessions for their leadership, expecting them not to lecture but to involve the others in discussion through problem raising and questioning. In an atmosphere of high tension, the first of these sessions took place with the student leaders compulsively reading aloud the pages of notes they had taken from the text material. Each was bent on displaying to me the fact that he or she had done the requested work thoroughly; no one else in the room was involved in any way. Politely silent, each sat through the delivery without interruption.

At the end of the three-hour class I explained again what I had in mind, expecting that—in some ways—the contrary example would have made it clearer. It did not alleviate their apprehension. The next week the stereotypic performance was repeated. When my obvious unhappiness deepened, I had an open rebellion on my hands: a strong request for lectures from me. They *needed* a traditional authority dispensing knowledge, a role that I could not provide at that time. Consequently, we adapted and revised our procedures to an ineffective compromise, and, having learned my lesson, I taught no more until the following summer, under very different and supportive circumstances. By that time, I was beginning to be reasonably functional, and guiding a laboratory course in counseling was somewhat within my renewed capabilities.

My error-ridden trials were not yet over. For me, simply living required the retrieval of all basic skills. Whether physical or intellectual, each was demanding, but the most difficult of these were thinking and writing. Unwilling to accept my losses and go on from there, I insisted on believing that I (who had authored or co-authored a number of published books) was perfectly capable of functioning as I had in the past. Out of sheer *chutspah* and mad fantasy, I took on a contract I had no reason to believe I could fulfill, spent nervous, drawn-out hours, days, and months in tense anxiety building an inappropriate and shaky structure on the typewriter, and grieved over its failure to stand. The outcome was not a unified, professional product; I was embarrassed. I was sure that I could never have performed so badly before my illness, but I could not do better at that time. Would I *ever* be able to?

Later I came to realize how important it had been for me to try to fulfill the assignment and meet the deadline. Instead of just an expression of simple ineptitude, the experience had been one of invaluable trial and practice in some of the processes that I needed to relearn. I researched and wrote exactly as I walked and swam—to revivify paralyzed skills—but I would probably not have done them so steadfastly, worked so hard at their retrieval, if I had not promised other people that I would.

This intellectual failure was the psychic equivalent of a physical one which occurred several months later. Because I was so unsteady on my feet, I tried to learn to fall—if not with grace, at least with ease—and much of the time I had succeeded in landing without injuring myself. The fear of clumsiness, of hurting myself in public, is always humiliating, but the fear of embarrassing others is even more so. Not everyone reacts the same way, however. One day when I was hurrying to catch a BART train for a meeting with my daughter, I went down suddenly and hard on a hillside sidewalk and sat there weeping bloodily. The homeowner gardening in his front yard beside me was not at all embarrassed. He called the ambulance, and his wife, noisily conferring with him in another language, brought me a hot cup of tea to drink from a lovely porcelain cup until it had arrived. The injury required nothing more than eight stitches through my eyebrow, but it was both a shock and a reminder.

I can describe where I am today physically as I have tried to discuss the stages lived through since my illness. Many times I have thought that I had reached a permanent plateau with emerging peaks of achievement visible above but far too sharp and steep for me to believe they were accessible. And many times, spurred by some outward pressure or my own pulsing motivation, I have pressed on and found myself, stumbling and panting, coming on a higher obstacle. There is *always* higher ground, and one person's achievement is never the same as another's.

As I grew better, I came to know that I was not out of control and that my image of myself—my stance of hopelessness and helplessness or my determination—could affect my healing body. I have not "recovered," if recovery means return to where and what I was before. Have I been victimized? Yes, I still have that sense—to a certain degree—but it is mitigated by my belief that I have acted powerfully in my own behalf and, by doing so, that I have changed my view of life. I know that if I hold self-destructive beliefs, accept them, and utilize them, I am responsible for their effects. I have had to approach each experience, each opportunity, even the negative and bizarre, as the origin of functional wisdom. I have had to learn to dwell in ragged, adaptive incomprehension, knowing the pieces would be joined in good time.

11 ⤳

EMERGENCY

My soul, like some heat-maddened summer fly,
Keeps buzzing at the sill. Which I is *I?*
A fallen man, I climb out of my fear.

—THEODORE ROETHKE

It is said that, when the Buddha first had his
enlightment, he was asked, "Are you a God?"
"No," he replied. "Are you a saint?" "No."
"Then what are you?" And he answered, "I *am*
awake."

In a dark time, the eye begins to see . . .

The disciples of Carl Jung believe that for all humans there are
three principal stages of potential psychosocial development.
These have an archetypal pattern. The first is the *unconscious*
perfection, the wholeness and unity, of innocence in childhood. The second is the *conscious imperfection* of middle life
and the awareness of duality and the separation and differentiation between inner and outer worlds. The third, old age's
conscious perfection, is the achievement of reconciliation between those two worlds and a state of *satori* or personal enlight-
enment. With the loss of memory, I had regressed beyond

childhood to prenatal unconsciousness and a state of developmental chaos. I had to begin again, to encounter first inner and
then outer obstacles which challenged the will and the sense
of identity. I did not have to win from someone else or over
him or her; I had to battle undifferentiated, neutral forces
whose ominous powers only incidentally were directed at me.
Out of control, I trudged on. I had to retrieve my status at the
second of these stages.

If history (as Theodore Roszak has said) is incompatible with
the transcendence of self or society, then loss of the past should
have freed me from that "prefabricated" identity. The loss was
real, but such freedom is an illusion. Others may have chosen
to shuck what has gone before as if it were a worn snake skin,
but that repudiation is never complete. *Volunteering* for the
loss cannot be that effective, and when the past is involuntarily
and truly gone, the unsolicited situation is quite different. The
chasm is not to be filled at will, and the bridging present is
never lived without awareness of the lack of supports below.

The outcomes of any experience—their effects and their
meaning—are not determinable by a standardized test mea-
surement; if we have learned what is not, for social or political
reasons, being measured, we are assumed not to have learned
anything. The knowledge I have recently gained *of* sickness
and health contains a specific element, both smaller and less
penetrating, *about* them. William James described the difference, pointing out that scientific methods in the West imply
objectivity and generalizability. They develop the latter
"about" while knowledge *"of"* is the domain of *individual*
consciousness and, as such, is indescribably valuable to the
person.

For all of its commonalities of experience, mending is the
expansion of personal meanings, the extension of contact, of

that consciousness that is growth in the midst of limitation and curtailments. That task became easier and easier for me as I gained courage from the evidence of change. The landscape around me has changed because *I* have changed. Belief in the body's capability became stronger; the cycle was self-reinforcing. I can say, as Norman Cousins wrote after his own recovery from grave illness, that

> I have learned never to underestimate the capacity of the human mind and body to regenerate—even when the prospects seem most wretched. The life-force may be the least understood force on earth. William James said that human beings tend to live too far within self-imposed limits. It is possible that these limits will recede when we respect more fully the natural drive of the human mind and body toward perfectibility and regeneration. Protecting and cherishing that natural drive may well represent the finest exercise of human freedom.*

To be *cured* is passive; it originates beyond the body, in other people and other forces. Its beginning and continuing processes are external. It is not the same as *healing,* for (as Cousins was in his mending) *I* must be involved if I am to heal. I must work with myself and acknowledge my freedom to make choices, to search for and to find a way of life compatible with what I am and what I wish to be. I have had to decide, as all adults do, how *I* am going to act, not just *re*act to another's directions. I am on my own again—the chooser and the choice implementor.

Fritjof Capra has discovered, in applying the New Physics to an understanding of the human psyche, that the individual

*Norman Cousins, *Anatomy of an Illness as Perceived by the Patient* (New York: Norton, 1979), p. 48.

is not unidimensional. There are at least three levels to be reckoned with: those of *ego* or *self-image;* those of *existential concern* with life and death; and those of the *transpersonal self* in the context of the whole cosmos. What is emerging today is a world view of the person that is organic, holistic, and ecological—a rediscovery that can be directly applied to health and to healing.

Illness is no exception to the rule expressed by Simone de Beauvoir that

> no factor becomes involved in the psychic life without having taken on human significance, it is not the body-object described by biologists that actually exists, but the body as lived in by the subject . . . it is not nature that defines; it is she [the person] who defines by dealing with nature on her own account in her psychic life.*

I know now that I am disabled, that I will not regain *all* my balance, my memory, my sight, my hearing. I accept it as I could not earlier. I could not pass as "normal" when the observable facts are incompatible with the claims I would be making. There are no simple ways to keep myself secret or to avoid the interpretations of unknowing observers. (But some are not too difficult—e.g., when going out after dark without my cane, arriving on the arm of a friend, then remaining seated for much of the evening and departing similarly unobtrusively supported.)

I came to feel, as Erving Goffman has suggested that all stigmatized persons may come to feel, that accepting and respecting myself destroys the need for concealment. Yes, my

*Simone de Beauvoir, *The Second Sex* (New York: Bantam, 1949).

social identity has changed from the whole and usual, but I do not see it reduced to a tainted, discounted, discredited one. Self-disclosure permits adaptive action. As I had quickly learned, there is indeed a "disclosure etiquette." If I whine, I will be avoided. If I attempt what others believe I will fail at doing, I will make them tense and nervous in my presence. But if I make them comfortable because I present myself as relaxed and self-confident, they will allow me to take chances and to manage for myself without dependence on others or without their feeling obliged to offer intrusive help.

Help offered has real complexities. Whether or not at a given moment it is actually needed, its availability may be greatly appreciated—even when it is seen as an encroachment on privacy and a presumption. Offering aid may create the social need for acceptance. But accepting it may make the prideful needy break out in sweat from humiliation at the same time that the act is a real gift to the extender.

Last summer at the University of Victoria I told about my illness because my class was curious. (A stigmatized person can even be approached by strangers at will, providing only that they present themselves as sympathetic to the plight of the person they are addressing.) Good will in this form is not always easy to cope with. Individual members had asked—informally, outside of the classroom—if I had had an accident, and it seemed simplest to take time to explain briefly to them all. My lack of awareness of their perception of the handicap and concern about the mystery was a mark of my distance from it by that time. I no longer thought about my disabilities; I simply managed them. I was over the trauma and markedly functional again. Disregard was not an attempt at concealment; it was a manifestation of the reorganization of my self-perception. I had become sufficiently detached, the condition taken in stride (if an unsteady one) to be unwilling to deal with my new social identity.

More than anything, each of us needs to be recognized by qualities other than our disabilities. Handicaps, whatever they are, are only a part of the person.

Should the disabled person, then, make a systematic effort at the re-education of the "normal" person, present convincing evidence that, in spite of appearances, underneath it all he or she is still a fully functioning human being? There is a masochistic element to this endeavor, but whether it is stronger than that in hiding and avoiding I do not know. We all want to forget, to ignore the unforgettable, and when this happens for brief periods of time we come back to our selves with shock and dismay.

Perhaps the trick, the necessity, is to identify one's own person and own roles for oneself. It is to insist not only on the retention of this privilege but also on the right to idealize—to denominate what *might be* as well as what *is* or clearly *can be.* It is the belief in oneself that is absolutely necessary because no one else knows or *can* know; I alone have the data, the access to what really is. But if others define me in terms of their observations and expectations, I am falsely pressured to fulfill them, to become what they believe is there instead of what I know I am.

The consequences of these pressures can be dreadful. When it is laid out by others, for instance, their role definition may be fixed and negative. A social myth does not describe a real situation; those who believe it try to bring about what it declares to be already existing. The myths about disability become reality when they are believed and internalized. These beliefs may include the expectation that the cripple be crippled both physically and psychically, that the injured, maimed, or ill stay that way and sustain an other-defined image of themselves. As the price of social survival, the disabled find themselves expected to maintain, to remain as diagnosed and labeled, even when they are aware of changing and their own translation of that awareness into activating hope. I may have left the world of the whole, but does it matter? That world is occupied only by abstractions and ideals, not by human beings. It is not a real world. There is *no one* without limitation, flaw, inadequacy, partiality, or fragmentation.

Believing in my physcal and intellectual limitations the first year of my recovery, my older daughter did more than stand by supportively: she took on many of the subdivisions of my domestic roles (and even some quasi-professional ones such as writing to colleagues to answer letters or give progressive reports). By the end of the second year, in our reversed roles, she was becoming impatient and rejected my diagnosis of current limitations as well as my fluctuating belief in absolute recovery. Like the old Avis Rent-A-Car ads, she thought that not being first in the field should make me try harder. She was bound to do less and force me on my own. There was nothing grand about the package being handed over; it was filled with the ordinary matters of grocery shopping, getting the car serviced, learning to sew again, cleaning my apartment, and taking over my financial responsibilities.

She thought that I was feeling sorry for myself and not working actively enough at recovery. I did not agree with her; I was trying to be realistic about my timing and my expectations as to what I could accomplish in each step on this long passage to health. But she would have none of it, and her scolding urgency made me laugh with appreciation and pleasure. She cared for me. Still, she could not know how far I had come since the ride home from the hospital—the growth of my peaceful conviction of progress. Her planned confrontation, with the two of us sitting in the parked car side by side, was an enactment of Goffman's lines:

> We lean on these anticipations that we have, transforming them into normative expectations, into righteously presented demands.*

As time went on, I took on more outside of my domestic sphere, playing out a rather weird mix of public bravado and private timidity. As I have recorded here, I sometimes succeeded and sometimes did not. (And when I did not, I learned to believe that, at the time, the attempt was necessary and the outcome unimportant. What mattered was the process undertaken, the revival of lost skills. I would not be humiliated out of practice and future trial. I was going to be a functional, competent person again, both privately and professionally, and testing myself—over and over again—was a necessary, if often discouraging, part of that progression.)

Since my illness I have dreamed only two or three times— in attacks of anticipatory anxiety about some professional task, some public appearance, to be accomplished the next day. Journals I kept long ago report that, in earlier life, nightly images had constantly ornamented my sleep. They have not reappeared in this new version of consciousness. But the illusive power to imagine and create has partially returned; once again it exists to be employed in the waking hours, although access to it is still both random and arbitrary.

It seems to me that the loss of some sensory capacities, some reduction in receivership, may lead to a kind of superdiscrimination of others. With hearing and eyesight diminished, I am more attuned to subtle differentiation of smell and taste; the

*Erving Goffman, *Stigma: Notes on the Management of Spoiled Identity*, p. 2.

touch of my skin is a greatly enhanced pleasure. (When I swim, I am aware of the movement of muscle and the stroke of flowing water against the surface of my body. Walking, I am conscious of the wind against me.) My eyes and ears have grown skins that I have learned to live with, to sense through and around. Just by being, I am learning to reach what I wish to see and to hear. I had encountered reality undisguised by words, but now those words, which had become unhinged and unrelated like drifting constellations, once more are patterned and accessible.

I still have some areas of amnesia. I think there may even be some element of choice involved in what is not recovered, or perhaps it is that people tend not to remind me of what has been negative in the past. If connections are made, I usually have to make them myself. And when "bad" things are let go, a reminder can be a real shock—so much so that I do not always take the word of others. When I pay attention to it, my memory may be largely reliable from day to day, but it is totally unpredictable. I must take notes and post messages to myself in ways I am sure that I have never done before.

I will always be trying the doors of memory. Some will spring open when pressed; others will not—and I will live forever in a domain partly sealed and inaccessible. Like a powerful phoenix, my knowledge is still struggling to emerge, knowledge more than cumulative, also reconstructive but with some of the portions obsolete and hence discarded. With no past, both present and future begin today. The present is all there is. What is here is what there is to be experienced. The present is my location now. The limitations have been transcended: there are other more important things to think about. I can chant "Pamela's Peyote Song" and feel its reality within me:

Freedom I am,
Spirit I am!
I am the Infinite within my soul.

I can find no beginning;
I can find no end.
I am; I am!

Can we humans choose for ourselves if we believe ourselves *unable* to do so? Surely, if we are to choose, we must know that we can. Freedom exists functionally only when its existence is recognized and believed in. Psychological barriers are more comprehensive, more enclosing, than social ones.

Waiting, hoping, and despairing, being and doubting—these were the years of recovery. Except for the first few months I was home from the hospital, the waiting has not been static, not negative; it has burgeoned and has been amplified with hope, even when my rational mind denied its rationality. Accepting my vulnerability was somehow admitting defeat. To acknowledge a wound or a weakness may be fatal, may make destruction inevitable. But an "endless" holding battle has to end. The real survivor must return to life, to the acceptance of vulnerability.

Coming across an old Protestant hymn, I was moved by its relevance to this period of my life:

Night, that made my eyes to see,
Death, that gave my life to me.

If I suffer from my lacks, I also feel elation at changes, at what I have become—new growth, shapes, intentions, awareness, and access. In health we can voluntarily stuff ourselves into figurative boxes, enjoying the sense of boundaries—real, separating, but not distancing—that allow the self to be alone. Or we can choose the alternative: we can return to interaction and the social world. My "rebirth" was like the beginning that Wordsworth imagined: "a sleep and a forgetting"; "not in utter nakedness, and not in entire forgetfulness" I have come back to participation and trial. From the beginning of my recovery, I have shown "This is what I am"—a limited, deficit, striving self—and have known that I must find a way for this being, still transient, still emergent, to be received and accepted.

Like the rest of the natural world, I have grown for no reason, hearing in my silence the shadowed sound of my own calling. I have developed, watching every step, every shift, with self-absorbtion, evidence to support hope for the future. *Finis origine pendet*—"the end depends upon the beginning." I had begun to mend; therefore, I would be mended.

I have taken up residence again in the multidimensional planes of my mind. When one emerges from forgetfulness, there is a quality of ascent, even when that ascent is seen as circular, containing the possibility of re-entry into the underworld of unconsciousness. I have moved from the blank void to multimeaninged objects and form. From being cornered and confined, I have found an ecological self-consciousness, a holistic vision of the on-going, worldwide life processes in synergetic combination, processes with which I know myself to be fused and integrated.

Can there be a valid establishment of the image of the recuperative, the rehabilitated—those who have been attacked and have survived, emergent in new adaptive form? If I were to attempt a typology of stages of recovery, it would not be as neatly sequential as that of Elisabeth Kübler-Ross's formulation for the dying. Some of the same elements would appear, though, as fairly distinct phenomena: transitions from *denial* or *disbelief; anger* and *active frustration; bargaining* through compliance and cosmic wheedling (although my vision of the Almighty did not allow me to do this); debilitating *depression* and discouragement as evidence mounts of lasting—perhaps permanent—limitations; and, finally, *acceptance* (which for the ill or injured does not mean withdrawal or the abandonment of feeling but, instead, the appearance and growth of stabilizing belief in the capacities that have endured or have been newly developed. Acceptance is a valued destination for recovery only when it is not giving up.) Each of these stages is interwoven with recurrent hope and the belief that some valid meaning inheres in what is experienced.

Such a list is inadequate for generalization, however, for like each death, each recovery is individual. The specific person in a specific sociophysical environment responds dynamically to the opportunity for regained health, perception, and power. I —the multirole writer of these words—am an idiosyncratic integration. Together, our lives may be generalizable into remote abstractions, but each separate one is not. I have recorded this portion of my life to understand it more deeply and to share it. It is mine, but here it is also given to others, a typescript overrun as it may be with disorderly productivity. I have not rid myself of "intellectually gaseous words"—as Alan Watts referred to *mind, soul,* and *spirit*—because they are integral to the experience. If I am to communicate what is private, I must depend on the mutuality of public language.

Today the urgencies of the immediate once more apply to the service of what may be. I had not given life up, but, more, it had not given me up either. It is not I who have been asking its meaning, but life which has questioned me about the meaning of *mine.* I was taught freedom through an apprenticeship in dispossession; I learned to let go by being forced to try it. This was the "Hour of Lead" that Emily Dickinson wrote about:

Remembered, if outlived,
As freezing persons recollect the Snow—
First—Chill—then Stupor—then the letting go.

I had learned to stop defining myself in terms of the past, learned to accept the rebuilding and the new architectural designs. Those new designs are the difference, for our whole knowledge of the world is self-knowledge. Alter the self and its instruments and the knowledge that is received changes. My disorganization has yielded to a symbolic reordering. I have become aware, profoundly, personally, of what Jascha Kessler has called "our delusion that we are rational in pursuing only the rational itself." I want to go forward now, but not in a linear way, not solely in an intellectual way. And I am no longer planning for arrival. The journey, not its ending, is the goal.

Robert Jay Lifton and Eric Olson have described the survivor as one who has traveled into the land of death and has become seer and prophet and healer through a process of transformation:

> The image is of the survivor as creator; the one who has known disintegration, separation, and stasis now struggling to achieve a new formulation of self and world.*

While I am neither seer nor prophet nor healer, that creative struggle continues for me. I have gained a knowledge of basic matters and have a most synoptic vision of life, an emergency redeemed in the coils and circuits of the brain, the tight, meandering blood, strength and movement in muscle and heart. My breath and my body's beat confound me. I have learned, too, the mysterious dimensions of relationship and

*Robert Jay Lifton and Eric Olson, *Living and Dying*, p. 122.

support: oh, let us then be *present* to one another! How much we need ontological communion!

Raymond Moody, Jr. wrote of life after "death" that those who underwent this experience were in "remarkable agreement" as to what they had learned from it: the importance of the cultivation of human love, an end of the fear of death, and a need for new goals and principles through which and for which they were determined to live. (Not one of his subjects referred to the experience of heaven or hell.) Without experiencing death literally, I nevertheless shared these insights.

Escape from loneliness, disability, and death is not escape from their actuality; it is escape from the *fear* of them. Like Admiral Byrd alone in the Antarctic, I had to transcend reason and to realize that despair was groundless. I have come further, for anyone who has been isolated or restricted in movement or thought breathes in awareness of expansion and freedom with every intake of air. I have found myself in the presence of truth I had not been able to recognize before. I have been through a time of radical solitude, found my own labyrinth and wound within. Emerging, I have been caught into transitions of oneness, serenity, elation, depression, and anger, as well as generalized sensual and emotional expansion. I have glimpsed the oblivion philosophers call an absurdity; I have drunk from the river of silence and have begun to learn to sing again.

I have lost my migraine attacks, and I have gained new sounds through a lengthened range of hearing. Time has adjusted; in this slowed present I have become more aware of interval and occupancy. I have grown the habit of taking pleasure from each day. My focus has been deeply altered; I am much more aware of my need for others and their needs for me. Able or disabled, we are together in this tyrannical matrix of space and time, of object, of action, and of love. I know that

I have a body, but I am not my body alone; its confines cannot cripple me.

For many of us, our imagination creates death as an image which shapes our perception of being in this world—sometimes adaptively and sometimes not. The capacity to live is contracted by the fear of death. I believe I have lost this fear forever. I retain my Nabokov landscape of that fabled experience: "windows giving upon a continuous world, a rolling corollary, the shadow of a train of thought." But it is alien and distant, unreal.

If walking or climbing, thinking or remembering require more energy and attention for me than in the past, the physical or intellectual effort is no horror. The awareness they require reminds me that I *can* do them, that I am *not* prevented by incapacity. I suspect that I once wanted a passe-partout for this vital journey, but there is none. This passage is not paid for in advance *or* after arrival, but earned along the way. I have crept toward health and function, and I will know that I have achieved them when I begin to worry about the conventional deterioration of aging. I am so aware of health and possibility that my new boundaries are not oppressive. Being a cripple is not a physical state; it is a way of thinking about yourself. So many times I have read or heard people say that human salvation and self-growth lie in the acceptance of what is, not in fight or resistance. I do not believe in such inertia.

There is a vision of the world won through hardship that is revivifying and supportive. There is always the need for courage; one may refuse to be crushed and destroyed. In plant or animal, submicroscopic or macroscopic creature, life has its own force; it is its own cosmos.

I have learned to accept my limitations, but I am less sure that I have been able to embrace the experience as a transcendent gift. There is more self-aggrandizement in that view than

I can manage. I do agree with Carolyn Vash, a professional woman crippled by polio early in adolescence, that the concept of *re*habilitation (as the word is commonly used) just does not apply; it is too regressive. Nobody who becomes disabled wants to or can be restored to a *previous* state. Too much has happened, too much that has tremendous validity as a stimulus toward psychological growth. Physical limitations—even intellectual ones—can be trivial compared to the access to realms of discovery and improvement which can still be experienced.

Experiencing the present at each step of the way, as I do today, I am still counting on improvement. I have built a new faith, and, in the process, I have learned to disguise my inadequacies, to hide my deficiencies of memory as far as possible by careful social preparation. (From a car window I saw an old friend whom I recognized without remembering his name or how I had known him. The driver beside me, who had known us both, filled in the connections before we reached our common meeting place.) I rarely discuss the disease; limitations observed by others must be taken to be innate, not acquired, characteristics.

Recovery should probably be defined in Freud's famous words: the implementation of the ability *to love* and *to work* —the love of my family, which I can now demonstrate in response to what they have so clearly shown me, and the love of a man who admits the reality of the damaging past, defines it in terms of moral courage, and refuses evidence of its continuation. The ability to work is still in process: as I have learned to drive, to shop, to find my way home and elsewhere, I have tried to relearn sewing and cooking. I am still unable to teach or write without great stress and continual self-distrust, rejecting each step of research and expression, repeating each again and again.

I do not believe that I have returned to what I was before.

Every new start demands the cessation of the old. Nullification makes both rejuvenation and transformation possible. I may be a reconstruction of old constituents, but they have been modified and adapted. My personality has changed: I am, for example, less reactive and more accepting, less pressured and more tentative, no longer willing to choose stress for the sake of worldly achievement. I am much less ambitious and, so others tell me, much less anxious than I have been, much less bound by ordinary anxiety and, perhaps, much more in touch with the existential anxiety that accompanies the knowledge of personal freedom and its limitations.

I believe that I have come in touch with the ultimate reality. I do not believe in immortality, in life after death in the conventional sense, but I do believe in an indestructible and timeless core within each personality.

I have mourned, have learned to abandon the defensive denial.* I remember—and will remember, whatever of the trauma I forget—being loved comprehensively, completely. Wonder will not disappear. I am here, twice-born, changed, emergent—like the recurrent images of rebirth in the oldest religious traditions. I can say to the dark, questioning philosopher of Ecclesiastes, "*I* knoweth the spirit of man that goeth upward."

*The ability to put aside the past voluntarily is a valuable gift. I am reminded of a Zen story of two monks who were traveling together by the side of a river when they heard the cries of a woman caught in the current and drowning. One of the men plunged into the water, seized hold of her, and carried her to safety on the shore. The two men resumed their journey as if nothing had happened. Much of the day passed before his companion suddenly spoke up and accused the rescuer of having contaminated himself by touching a woman.

"But *I* put her down six hours ago," the accused man responded.

BETHANY'S EPILOGUE

Before the events described in this book—catastrophic illness, disability, and recovery—the author was an ambitious, athletic, intellectually gifted woman in vigorous mid-life. Her children grown, her career and life were her own. In demand as a lecturer and consultant, Elizabeth Léonie Simpson traveled throughout North America and much of the rest of the world.

The illness began like a flu: her body ached with a fever. Suddenly she became delirious. On Halloween, in 1974, she was admitted to the hospital.

At the hospital, between white sheets in a strange, glassed isolation room, she looked macabre. Her head was swollen with infection, her cheeks sunk with fever, her eyes bright with hallucinations. Talking too brightly, automatically, she was not conscious. She sang snatches of songs, in Spanish.

As I watched by her bedside, swathed myself in protective clothing, her talk became more childish. She—who had been authority figure, provider, poet, scholar, and prose stylist, who had been an original personality—became dull and tense as a sulky six year old.

Finally, before the coma, the vibrations changed again. She was still speaking, but the sense had become nonsense, gibber-

ish, just jumbled sounds. The doctors called it "word salad." In the two months spent in hospitals watching for my mother to return to her senses, I never heard a more descriptive phrase of medical jargon.

After a long coma she awoke. She was infantile, weak, and incontinent. She was also mentally disoriented. While comatose, she had still been the same person she was previously— nearly dead but the same. That illusion was shattered when she regained consciousness. She was no longer swift-minded and sharp-tongued. Traits that had once been amusing—absent-mindedness and a vivid imagination—were distorted into list-lessness and fantasy.

This book is about how she regained not only her faculties, but her gifts. She accepts life now, grateful for what it offers without begrudging what it costs. Human crises always have a purpose. In my mother's case, they have enabled a rigid personality to make radical changes. That is what I believe happened.

She had survived, a hero for defeating death. Powerful although enfeebled, she re-created herself in another image. Significantly, she did not strive to become again the woman she once was. She learned to love the past, which—in her personal history—had always been adversary. This has made her a very different woman. Her story is a cocoon from which emerged an unexpected kind of creature: a spinner who can connect the past to the future, as they must be connected, in living.